6. 9. '86

Bogie
and
Me

A Love Story

Bogie *and* Me

Verita Thompson

with
Donald Shepherd

St. Martin's Press
New York

BOGIE AND ME. Copyright © 1982 by Verita Thompson
with Donald Shepherd. All rights reserved. Printed in
the United States of America. No part of this book may
be used or reproduced in any manner whatsoever
without written permission except in the case of brief
quotations embodied in critical articles or reviews. For
information, address St. Martin's Press, 175 Fifth
Avenue, New York, N.Y. 10010

Library of Congress Cataloging in Publication Data

Thompson, Verita.
  Bogie and Me.

  1. Bogart, Humphrey, 1899-1957. 2. Thompson,
Verita. 3. Moving-picture actors and actresses—United States—
Biography. 4. Unmarried couples—United States—Biography. I.
Shepherd, Donald. II. Title.
PN2287.B48T47   791.43'028'0924 [B]   82-5582
ISBN 0-312-08738-1   AACR

Design by Kingsley Parker

First Edition

10 9 8 7 6 5 4 3 2 1

To Grace Robbins (Harold's better half),
who
pushed me to get my story told

and to

Barney Leason, Gaye Tardy, Ray Crosett,
and Esther Richmond, who
pushed me in the right direction

Contents

A section of photographs follows page 82.

The dialogue presented here has been reconstructed from my journal and from memory. Bogie was a man of memorable speech patterns and thorny words, so the dialogue attributed to him will be substantially what he said and very often exactly the way he said it.

—V.T.

Preface

In the twenty-five years since Humphrey Bogart's death, he has become a cult figure. And justifiably so. Bogie was an enormously fascinating man. He was a vivacious, sensitive, bittersweet, and secretly gentle iconoclast who was very much in touch and in sympathy with the human condition and who never let those around him forget that they, too, had feet of clay. I loved him dearly (too much, in fact, to marry him when he asked me to), and I'm proud that he chose to share part of his life with me. My years with Bogie were among the loveliest, zaniest, most exciting, and memorable ones of my life. Hardly a week passes that I'm not reminded of him by one of our old friends visiting my restaurant or by seeing a television rerun of one of the pictures we worked on together. I savor those memories.

In recent years, articles concerning my fifteen-year love affair with Bogie have been appearing in national tabloids. One article even made reference to a young would-be actor who was calling himself Victor Humphrey and claiming to be the illegitimate son of Bogie and me. I'm not surprised that someone tried to capitalize on the revelation of our affair; sensational stories leave one vulnerable to such opportunists.

Our affair was not unknown to many movie-colony insiders—and to be truthful, I have no objection to the general public learning about it. I do object, though, to the distorted and unsavory context in which the affair has been publicly revealed; a manner—not the fact—that is an embarrassment to me in the eyes of my casual friends, acquaintances, and business patrons. I never know when someone will come into my restaurant to show me the latest tabloid containing an article with a banner headline like, "I Was Bogie's Secret Love!" and with photographs of Bogie and me. That's exactly what happened just a few months ago; the article contained no by-line, thus making it seem that I had written it. Now that's embarrassing!

Many biographies have been written about Bogie, and more will undoubtedly follow. I haven't been mentioned in any of them, but it's inevitable now that I will be; the tabloid stories are sure to come to the attention of future biographers, and owing to the sensationalism of such source material, I would become a sleazy footnote in Bogie's history and Bogie's image would be unjustly distorted by our apparently "unsavory" affair. That is, unless I tell our story fully.

For this reason, I haven't the slightest compunction about sharing my story with others, particularly with those of his fans who greatly admire him and who have a seemingly insatiable curiosity about him; indeed, I'm pleased that the day has come when one can be open and honest about such things. Those who have faced life squarely, who revere human dignity with compassion for the weaknesses of the human condition and who have truly loved and have been loved should find nothing sleazy or sordid about my relationship with Bogie. As for those who are prone to judge others by some Procrustean measurement of their own devising, well, to paraphrase Margaret Mitchell's Rhett Butler: frankly, my dears, I don't give a damn! Neither would Bogie. He loved needling the holier-than-thou. And he would have taken particular delight in knowing that twenty-five years after his death—through me—he was still sticking it to them.

He'd love it.

The growing ranks of Bogart fans will find this little-known side of Bogie's life interesting. And it is just and only that: one side of his life. I will relate relevant facts of his background and life as he related them to me over the years, but even so, this is simply a sketch, just one facet of a complex man drawn from my unique vantage point.

I traveled with Bogie at home and abroad. I was with him at the studios and on location for nearly all of the sixteen films he did from 1950 until his death—and a few of the films he made before 1950. And, yes, I shared many a bed with him, too. So this is a personal memoir, and I caution the reader not to expect movie reviews or dissertations on Bogie's films, which would be far beyond my expertise and the scope of this book. Some films and the making of them will be mentioned in passing, but anyone who's worked in the movie industry knows that it's assembly-line work and that, in time, one film blends into another until it's almost impossible to remember their titles, let alone specifics about the shooting of them. This is particularly true of Bogie's films, for as a contract player at Warner Brothers, he was forced to do one after another. And while their plots differed (well, sometimes), his parts didn't; it took a long time for Jack Warner to realize that Humphrey Bogart could do something more on screen than grow a beard, point a gun, and look menacing.

I intend to tell our story honestly—with no holds barred—the way Bogie might have himself. That was his style. It's mine, too. Like the rest of us, Bogie was human, but he never pretended otherwise. He could be an absolute pain in the ass at times—often, in fact. But he had unique and endearing qualities, and this book will celebrate the love, the laughter (lots of it), and the lust for life manifested in Humphrey DeForest Bogart. It's my way of saying to him, after all these years: here's looking at you, too, kid.

—Verita Thompson

Beverly Hills, California
Spring 1982

Part One

1

Spring 1944

The door to Bogie's studio dressing room at Warner
Brothers was ajar, so I didn't bother to knock. He was
sitting in a black-lacquered cane chair before the mirror of his corner dressing table, waiting. He looked, at
the moment, very much as he did on screen, a cigarette
dangling from his slightly parted lips, his brow wrinkled
like a basset hound's.

Gordon Bau, head of studio makeup, had already
finished with Bogie and was lounging on the couch of
the dressing-room alcove. I said hello to Gordon and
then introduced myself to Bogie. He didn't say a thing
or even look up at me. I had a makeup case in one hand
and partial hairpieces in the other, and Bogie kept staring at the damn hairpieces as though they were living
things he expected at any moment would crawl up my
arm or jump to his shoulder.

The mood of the scene fit the occasion. Through the
venetian blinds of the window above the couch where
Gordon sat, I could see that it was still raining like hell.
It was one of those cold, dark, and gloomy southern

California winter-spring days—the early spring of 1944 —but it was more somber in the dressing room than it was outside.

I told Bogie in as cheery a tone as I could summon that the fitting wouldn't take long.

"Okay, genius," he said, turning in his chair to face the mirror. "Let's get this thing over with."

He had given the word *genius* a particularly nasty twist, as only Bogie could, but I ignored the remark and got to work.

Jack Warner, the majordomo of Warner Brothers' Burbank studio, had issued an edict to Gordon Bau to do something about Bogie's hair. Up till then, makeup artists had been using fuller's earth to darken the bald spot on the back of his head, but his hair was getting too thin for that and had begun receding at the temples. More extreme measures were called for. Warner wanted Bogie fitted with a toupee and had ordered that it be worn at all times. Actually, he wouldn't need a full frontal toupee for a couple of years yet, but he was in need of a partial one. My job was to design it, and Warner Brothers would give it a screen test to see how it filmed.

The order rankled Bogie. He didn't like being told what to do—particularly by Jack Warner. He and Jack had been at war for years, but Warner was the boss and had a contract to prove it, so Bogie had little recourse.

There was no doubt in my mind about how Bogie would play the scene. He had already told Warner, very loudly: "I'm not going to prance around the studio with a fucking *beaver* on my head!" This remark was trumpeted along the studio grapevine, to everyone's amusement, and caused a member of the studio art department to draw Bogie a risqué cartoon depicting a man, presumably from the makeup department, with a patch of hair in his hand and running from a naked woman, who is chasing him and holding that portion of her anatomy from which the patch of hair had been snatched. Bogie's personal moral code usually didn't allow for off-color jokes or such licentious artwork, but under the circumstances, this personalized cartoon amused him, and it hung in his dressing room for all to see until he grew tired of it and gave it to me. I still have the damn thing; it's not well drawn, but it brings back amusing memories.

Bogie made an issue of the necessity of wearing a toupee and of Jack Warner's orders in general. He knew, of course, that it was for his own good; he just didn't like being told. And since the order to wear a toupee at *all* times was not written into his contract, Bogie later antagonized Warner by strolling around the studio with neither his toupee nor his hat, deliberately showing off his bald spot and receding hairline.

So I had no doubt that Bogie would act as though I were the embodiment of Jack Warner's control over him and the instrument (to paraphrase Bogie) of Warner's diabolical plot to make him look like a fag. And sure enough, Bogie gave me hell, grumbling throughout the fitting, swearing dark oaths against the makeup department in general and Warner and me in particular. "It's not enough for movie moguls and broads like you that a man has dedicated years to learning his craft," he growled. "He's gotta be *pretty,* too!"

Bogie pulled out all the sarcastic stops. And no one could be more sarcastic. I don't recall everything he said during his nonstop grumbling, but he growled at considerable length about how the little pieces of French lace and hanks of hair I was "glueing" on his head were going to improve his acting ability. "Next time Jack Warner wants to see me, I'll just have this muff sent over to his office by messenger and let him talk to *it*. Their goddamn IQs are about the same," Bogie said. And at one point he suggested that I bring his hairline down to his eyebrows to give him the Neanderthal look of a movie mogul. He was funny as hell, but I didn't dare laugh.

I kept my own remarks light, making a couple of wisecracks that I thought were funny. He kept glancing menacingly at me in the mirror. He was one hell of an actor. He bristled with hostility in his manner and his expression. Bogie always told aspiring young actors not to act. "Just feel what you want to be and you'll be it," he told them. Bogie was obviously feeling hostile. I was standing between Gordon Bau and him, so Gordon couldn't see Bogie's eyes in the mirror. Bogie had the most expressive eyes of any person I've known. Now they were flashing with anger, and Gordon Bau was probably bracing himself for the inevitable explosion from the force Bogie was building in the room. But every so often Bogie would glance at me in the mirror, and his eyes would say: "How we doing, ol' girl? We pulling this one off?"

When I finished, Bogie gave himself a long and critical look in the mirror. I packed my paraphernalia into the makeup case and was at the door, about to leave, when he sat back and said, "I'm not being paid to look *handsome,* you know."

"I just came in to fix your *hair,*" I said. "There's not a damn thing I can do to help your *face.*"

Bogie suddenly stood up. His abrupt action startled Mr. Bau, who looked at Bogie wide-eyed and expecting the worst. I half-turned, ready to bolt from the room like a bat out of hell, but Bogie flashed that crooked grin of his and said, looking me up and down as though for the first time, "Well, well. You *are* a sassy li'l broad, aren't you?"

"I can handle tough guys like you," I said with a kidding tone.

"Yeah. I'll bet you can. What'd you say your name is?"

"Peterson, Verita Peterson."

"*Verita?* What the hell kind of name is *that?*" Before I could reply, he said, "Peterson, huh? I'll call you Pete. I call the captain of my boat Pete. I can remember that name. See you at the screening, Pete."

What I have just described is, as nearly as I can recall, exactly what happened that spring day in 1944. What I have *not* related is that the scene was an elaborate rib we staged for Gordon Bau. One of the connotations of the word *rib* is to tease or make fun of, and it's usually used as a verb. But in show-business parlance, *rib* is more often used as a noun, and it can be defined as a little drama staged solely for the purpose of deceiving another person or persons, usually with humorous intent. I mention this because Bogie was one of the premier practitioners of the rib; it was so suited to his nature that had it not existed before him, he would have devised it himself. And in his hands, it was an art form, though it wasn't always considered funny by others. When a perverse mood stirred him, arising usually

from boredom, Bogie could pull ribs that often provoked fighting moods in his victims. And if they didn't
cool down and laugh at the situation, he'd dismiss them
and the incident by saying, "No sense of humor, huh,
ol' boy?"

Bogie had no tolerance for people who couldn't laugh
at themselves or who took themselves too seriously. To
him, the rib was a test of true character, a little existen-
tial Rorschach. If you couldn't see the humorous side of
the absurd provocation once it was revealed, then, to
Bogie's mind, you had lost touch with reality and the
human condition and were blinded by self-importance.

The rib that we pulled on Gordon Bau, however,
wasn't staged for laughs or as a test of character. I say
we because I was a party to it. We hadn't rehearsed it
or anything, so I didn't know exactly how Bogie was
going to play it, but he had set it up, and it was vital to
us that it work.

The fact is, Bogie and I had been lovers for two years
before that day when I walked into his dressing room
with the hairpieces. And we were both married at the
time. Neither of us was happily married, but in those
days, divorces were dehumanizing and lengthy ordeals
in which mental cruelty or infidelity had to be established in public hearings and the participants subjected
to scrutiny through the world press if they were celebrities. Each of us was destined for divorce at the time,
each on the trailing edge of an unsuitable marriage,
divorced in thought but not in fact. So we were having
an illicit and very dangerous affair.

The moral climate was one of the dangers we faced
in those early 1940s—a critical backwash from the

Roaring Twenties, when the fledgling movie industry had developed unchecked and had begun mirroring life in the raw. Politicians seized upon the attendant public outrage and would have been delighted to effect legislation governing the industry. To avert this, the movie industry pledged to police itself and thus formed a number of internal censorship bodies, of which the "Hays office" was probably the best known and most influential. As is generally the case when the pendulum of human events swings back, it swung to the opposite —and equally absurd—extreme, and the idea of common decency was carried to ridiculous lengths as Hollywood created a world without toilets, double beds, physical love, and the like.

Unfortunately, the fantasy world created by the Hays office and others was imposed on the real lives of the industry's stars by self-appointed moral guardians like columnists Hedda Hopper and Louella Parsons, among others, who could quite literally destroy a career by public disclosure of an actor's private life. Had the public learned that Bogie was having an affair, he could have become instant box-office poison. I would have had less to lose, but my little career was as important to me as Bogie's was to him; I would have been barred from the studios, as was their practice at the time, had my relationship with him become widely known. Worse, though, was the incontrovertible fact that I alone could be responsible for ruining Bogie's career, a burden that grew heavier and heavier as our relationship deepened.

We were playing a dangerous game for high stakes, and we were playing it like a couple of fools. I was young and crazy and in love. And while I won't speak for Bogie, he was not one who shied away from risk taking and wouldn't even seriously entertain the fear that I occasionally expressed regarding the chances we were taking. He used to say constantly, "Hell, Pete, no matter what happens, they can't say we haven't lived." The implication was always that the life we were leading—and our love—was more important than, or worth, the consequences we might have to pay. At the time, Bogie was married to his third wife, Mayo Methot (about whom I'll have more to say later); he had begun dating Mayo before he was divorced from his second wife, actress Mary Philips, and he had known Mary before divorcing his first wife, actress Helen Menken.

Despite the danger, our relationship continued, but it was a terrible strain on us both. Until that meeting in his dressing room at which Gordon Bau was present, we had to avoid meeting in public; so the purpose of the little drama we staged for Bau was to give us a legitimate and socially acceptable reason for being seen together. If I was hired as Bogie's hairdresser, it promised to take a great deal of strain from our lives.

Owing to a strong craft union and a very tight-knit studio group, there were no openings in the Warner Brothers makeup department, and free-lance hairstylists were seen by the union and the studio as interlopers. But I was tolerated for reasons that I'll go into later, and so when Jack Warner insisted that Bogie wear a toupee, Bogie saw it as an exploitable development. If he worked it right, he could not only produce an excuse for us to be together but also take secret delight in using Warner's own edict for purposes that would have given Jack Warner cardiac arrest had he known.

Bogie had purposely raised such hell at the prospect of having to wear a toupee that Gordon Bau was actually relieved when Bogie pointed me out to him one day and said, "What about getting that broad as my hairdresser?" Gordon would have preferred assigning someone from his own department, but if granting Bogie's offhand and seemingly spontaneous wish could resolve a tense situation, it would be to his and the studio's advantage to bring me in. And so Gordon called me, and Bogie and I pretended to be strangers. As a result, Gordon was happy; he could report back to Jack Warner that he had effectively handled what could have been a knotty problem. Bogie was so delighted with the "big rib" that he laughed his ass off for weeks afterward; he was like a kid whenever either of us mentioned it. I had never seen him so delighted with a rib; his only regret was that he couldn't tell anyone else about it. As for me, I was happy and relieved that we had both cause to be together and a flesh-and-blood witness who could testify that my association with Bogie was "recent" as well as strictly professional.

Until then, I had been hitting the bottle as hard as Bogie. I had been terrified. It was a subtle terror, like the slow realization that one is not stuck in mud but rather sinking in quicksand. Sure, I had stepped into the damn mess with my eyes open, but that didn't make it any less terrifying. Today, looking back on those times, I am absolutely amazed that either of us could have been so stupid as to take such chances. I say this with perfect hindsight, of course—for when I first met Bogie, I was swept away with the irresistible tide of our developing relationship, floating free—and gladly—from my mundane moorings and too euphoric even to imagine, let alone contemplate, the possibility of an undertow or its consequences.

2

Winter 1942

I had seen Humphrey Bogart around the Warner Brothers lot. I was free-lancing at nearly all the studios in those days, so I didn't see him often, but I liked what I saw. He seemed different from most of the actors I'd met, and I found him attractive; maybe it was his unaffected manner that made me take particular note. It wasn't his looks. He wasn't exactly handsome—though he had been in his earlier, Broadway-stage days—but he had rough-hewn good looks and a masculine, man's-man air about him. I found him sexy, particularly his eyes and mouth. He took no notice of me, of course, and I had no personal encounter with him until I was introduced to him by Ann Sheridan.

I had met Annie a few months earlier at Max Factor's on Hollywood Boulevard. She was with producer Henry Blanke (who produced several of Bogie's films, including *The Petrified Forest* and *The Maltese Falcon*), and they were choosing a wig for her to wear in one of Blanke's films. Annie and I established an immediate rapport; she was Irish and had a passion for Mexico and things Mexican, including the cuisine, which she loved and which she cooked very well. I'm half-Irish (my father) and half-Mexican, and I shared Annie's love for Mexican food and for cooking. We spent countless hours in the kitchen of her San Fernando Valley ranch house. She loved giving intimate dinner parties and usually cooked the dinners herself; I joined her in the cooking whenever I was around.

We later cooked for Bogie at Annie's, too, but the only dish for which he ever showed enthusiasm was my chili. One could fashion the most exotic cuisine for him, and he would only pick at it. He had little interest in food. He was a ham-and-eggs man—at least, that was what he usually ordered when he was dining out. It didn't matter whether he was in Los Angeles or New York or Rome or Paris or whether it was morning, noon, or night; it was usually the same: "Ham and eggs," he'd say, then he'd hold out his hand, palm up, and add, "eggs over easy," rotating his hand slowly, palm down, to demonstrate how the eggs should be turned. Like tugging at his earlobe, it was an unconscious and characteristic habit.

Annie and I got acquainted at Max Factor's by discussing the wig she was selecting. Some question regarding it had been posed by her or Henry Blanke, and I answered it. That was why I happened to be in Max Factor's that day; I was in the wig business.

I had first come to Hollywood under contract to Republic Studios as an "actress." I put the word in quotes because I didn't know a damn thing about acting and still don't, but that didn't seem to bother Republic. I had come to their attention as a runner-up in a Miss Arizona beauty contest, which I had entered on my own. My parents both died when I was young, and I was raised by my paternal grandparents in Arizona. My grandfather was a surgeon and quite wealthy. He spent most of his time lecturing at medical facilities like Johns Hopkins at home and abroad. I often traveled with him after my grandmother died, but I still managed to graduate from high school in Arizona and had entered the beauty contest because I thought it might be exciting. My grandfather was out of the country when Republic offered me a contract. I had finished school and had no immediate plans, so I thought the least I could get out of the offer was a paid vacation to Hollywood.

As did many other contract players of the day, I spent most of my time in Hollywood drawing my weekly check and waiting to be cast in a picture. The town was exciting in those days; there were always grand parties to go to, and I attended them all while I had the chance. When Republic finally put me in a picture, my acting career was short and not very sweet. It was a Western. I got the part because I had learned to ride horses quite well in Arizona, and I was one of the few actresses under contract who could. What I didn't know was that the studio didn't employ stunt riders—except for their stars. During the first day's shooting, I was required to do a particularly tricky bit of riding. I fell off the damn horse and broke my arm.

The plaster wasn't even dry on my cast (neither was the ink on the form I signed, releasing the studio of liability for the broken arm) when studio attorneys were scrutinizing the fine print in my contract with a magnifying glass and finding cause to release me from it as no longer being able-bodied. That made me mad as hell at Hollywood, so I left immediately for Mexico

City, where I planned to recuperate and sulk a lot.

And so I was sulking in the sunshine by the hotel pool shortly after my arrival when a small, elderly man with a kindly face and a thick French accent struck up a conversation with me—an extremity in a cast is always a good conversation opener. This fortuitous conversation changed the course of my life. The little Frenchman was an artisan, a maker of wigs and toupees of exceptional quality. When he had seen war clouds gathering in Europe, he fled to Mexico with an enormous quantity of French lace and hair from European nunneries—even today, French lace is the finest foundation for the making of wigs and toupees, and it wasn't available during World War II.

The Frenchman had cornered the market on French lace, but there wasn't much demand for his work or product in Mexico. The biggest and best market for his wares was Hollywood, and he was frantic to trade there, but it was wartime and he couldn't get the necessary papers for entry into the United States. He related his story to me when he learned where and how I had broken my arm. Then he suggested that I could be his Hollywood contact, and that as his agent I would get a percentage on any sales I made.

In the meantime, my grandfather had died and had left me a considerable inheritance. I'd made many valuable social contacts while I was in Hollywood, and I knew my way around, so I suggested instead that I invest capital in the venture. He agreed, and we formed a partnership; it was a fail-safe investment for me and a godsend for him. I bought an automobile, loaded it with wigs, falls, and toupees, and struck out for Hollywood again.

I struck out when I arrived in Hollywood. I discovered that the studio makeup departments were closed to me because I didn't have a cosmetologist's license. It was a union ruling. I was told that I could hire a cosmetologist to represent me, but I didn't like that idea at all; it would have cut into business profits and cut me out of valuable contacts I needed within the studios. So I went to beauty school, passed the state board examinations, and became a licensed hairdresser. I had looked upon the necessity of having a license as an obstacle, but it turned out to be a blessing. I learned the business, and it enabled me to design the wigs and toupees for the Frenchman, who remained in Mexico City, and to fit and apply them properly. The quality of our product opened doors in Hollywood that would otherwise have been closed to me, and so I began working with many female stars and such leading men as Charles Boyer, Gary Cooper, and Ray Milland long before I came to Bogie's attention.

After meeting Ann Sheridan at Max Factor's, I stopped in to see her one afternoon while making my rounds at Warner Brothers. She was just leaving to join a party on Stage 14 and invited me to join her. It was a wrap-up party, the kind usually thrown at the completion of a motion-picture shooting, and I believe it was for *Casablanca.* Annie was working on a sound stage nearby—*King's Row,* with Ronald Reagan, I think— and it wasn't unusual for friends working on nearby sets to drop in. Warner ground out so many films in those days that there always seemed to be a wrap-up party in progress. Anyway, having done a number of films together, Annie and Bogie were good friends, and so she attended the party.

Depending upon the producer and the film's impor-
tance, the parties could be lavish affairs, and this one
was. It was set up on a huge sound stage, with L-shaped
tables, catered food, an open bar, and a dance orchestra. The party was in full swing when Annie and I
arrived. People were coming and going all evening
long, but the crowd was always more than a hundred. We saw Henry Blanke sitting at a table with Jack
Warner, director Michael Curtiz, Gary Cooper, and
others, so we joined them. I took a seat next to Blanke,
and Annie was sitting across from us when Bogie
arrived.

Bogie looked around the sound stage for a moment
and then, upon seeing Annie and Blanke, headed
straight for our table. I knew that he and Annie were
friends and that one day I was bound to meet him; I
looked forward to it. As he neared the table, I watched
him approach and was intrigued to see that he was
staring directly at me, not taking his eyes from me for
a moment. It crossed my mind that I might be the
evening target for his notorious needling, but the
thought didn't unnerve me as it apparently did some in
Hollywood; I was too young and stupid to be insecure
and too thick-skinned to fear any barbs he might toss
my way.

When he got to the table, he glanced over at Blanke
and said—typically—"Where'd a creep like you find
such a good-looking broad?"

Before Blanke could answer, Annie looked up at him,
smiling, and said, "Which one of us two good-looking
broads are you referring to?"

Bogie laughed, patted Annie on the shoulder, and
took the seat next to her, across from me. "How you

doing, Annie?" he said. "Do you know this good-looking chick you're sitting across from?"

Annie introduced us, and that was about the last we saw of her; Bogie gave me his undivided attention for the rest of the evening. Well! I was flattered. And I was delighted to discover that, unlike many in Hollywood, he didn't talk about himself or his pictures or his acting. He wanted to talk about me. As I later learned, Bogie had a secure ego that didn't require self-inflation, and he had an insatiable curiosity about others. He asked me so many questions that he knew my entire life story before the evening ended. I told him why I had come to Hollywood: about the beauty contest, the broken arm, the Frenchman, the wigs, my grandfather. He said that his father had been a surgeon, too, a successful one in Manhattan, before he lost almost everything through bad investments.

True to his nature, Bogie spent half the evening kidding me and trying to find out the year I had entered the Miss Arizona beauty contest. I invoked my woman's prerogative and refused to tell him; this, of course, made him redouble his efforts to find out. Finally, I gave him a specific year: nineteen thousand.

"You sure it wasn't nineteen hundred?" he said.

Bogie never let anything like that go. Even as he lay dying, fifteen years later, he introduced me to his internist by saying, "Doc, this is Pete. She was a runner-up for the Miss Arizona beauty contest of nineteen thousand."

We had a bite to eat, but mostly we drank and danced the evening away. We must have danced for the better part of four hours. And as the booze began taking effect, Bogie started getting amorous and kissing my cheek as we danced. I was more than a little worried about this development; although Jack Warner had gone, many of the studio executives were still there. I finally said to Bogie, "You'd better stop that or you'll get us both in trouble."

"I know," he said, then, affecting an English accent, "but you're very, very tempting, my dear."

Naturally, Bogie had asked me about my husband, who was a film technician with another studio, and about our marriage. I told him honestly that it wasn't a good marriage for me. My husband was a good man, but he was a very cold one and a loner. He was a workaholic, too, and when he wasn't working, he was either playing poker or fishing with the boys. I was simply a convenience for him. When I married, I had considered giving up my business, but it was soon evident that I'd have nothing to do but sit at home and wait for one of his occasional visits if I did; my husband was seldom there.

I knew about Bogie's wife, Mayo; she was notorious among movie insiders, and Bogie was talking about divorcing her. I didn't know how bad and how dangerous their marriage was then. So we both had unhappy marriages, and that no doubt contributed to our mutual attraction. I felt very comfortable with Bogie, as though I had known him all my life. He later told me that he had felt exactly the same.

So our long romance began on Sound Stage 14, while we were dancing. In a movie, this would have been the big scene: lingering stares into the depths of one another's eyes; a thousand violins; that prefrontal-lobotomic expression that overwhelmed lovers get; Bogie whispering sweet nothings in my ear, poetic phrases about the blueness of my eyes. But this wasn't a movie.

As we danced into late evening, Bogie finally whispered to me, "You've got a great ass, ol' girl."

I had been around Hollywood long enough not to pretend shock at the remark; it struck me as humorous, and I laughed. Here we were, dancing to beautiful music on a grand Hollywood stage—like Fred Astaire and Ginger Rogers—and he throws me a low-down line like that. I could imagine how it would've gone over in a film flickering across the silver screens of middle America.

"That's really romantic, you sweet-talker," I said. "And what color are my eyes? No peeking."

"Blue," he said, "and don't change the subject."

"I'm glad you like my mind," I said. "That's where my brain is—in my ass."

Bogie laughed.

"I'm serious," I said. "That must be where my brain is or I wouldn't be dancing like this with you in front of all the studio brass."

"To hell with the creeps. And don't change the subject."

"I'm not accustomed to discussing my ass with strangers."

"I'm not a stranger," Bogie said, "I'm an ass man."

"You're also a little drunk."

"Not enough to forget that I'm an ass man."

And so the evening went—Bogie constantly teasing me, trying to shock me. We laughed and danced and drank, and that called for more laughing and dancing and drinking. It was nearly one o'clock in the morning when we finally left the party; Bogie loved parties and was usually the last to leave—unless the liquor ran out.

I had parked on the back lot, quite a distance from the sound stages. Bogie walked me to my car and asked how I could be reached the following day. I gave him my phone number. He kissed me good night and said he'd call the next day. Of course, everyone says that in Hollywood, but they rarely mean it and rarely do it. But I believed Bogie, and I drove away with my head spinning—and not just from drink.

3

Trench Coats and Shower Doors

Bogie called the next morning and asked me to meet him for lunch at the Smoke House, a restaurant on Lakeside Drive, across from Warner Brothers. I arrived at the appointed time, and he was already seated in a booth, martini in hand, waiting for me. He was always punctual. He deplored the habit of some celebrities— and some who thought of themselves as celebrities—of always being late for appointments, always keeping others waiting. To Bogie, this was symptomatic of going Hollywood, as he called it; he thought that wasting another person's time was the lowest of egotistical and unconscionable acts. And to my knowledge, he never kept anyone waiting, neither on the set nor for a personal appointment.

I slid into the booth beside him, and the first question he asked was whether I had enjoyed myself the evening before.

"Are you kidding?" I said. "I had a wonderful time. Of course I enjoyed myself. Did you?"

"Yeah," he said. "Listen, I didn't get out of line, did I, Pete?"

He asked the question almost apologetically. And he looked at me with genuine concern, waiting for my answer. I had to smile. Here was the needler, the tough guy, as he was known on the Warner Brothers lot, gravely concerned about whether he had insulted me or hurt my feelings.

"You were a gentleman," I said. "Not a perfect gentleman, but a gentleman."

He smiled. "A gentleman, huh? Well, don't let it get around. It could ruin my reputation."

We ordered lunch. Bogie ordered ham and eggs and another martini—a strange combination for anyone but Bogie; he was drinking too much in those days, especially martinis. Eventually (by the mid-1940s) they got the better of him and he had to give them up, switching to a drink he dubbed loudmouth—Scotch and soda—the drink he favored until his death. He called the cocktail loudmouth for obvious reasons—it loosened the tongue.

Bogie had a much-deserved reputation as a hard drinker. But he could hold it well. It was against his personal code of conduct to get falling-down drunk, to lose his dignity. There are those who will dispute this, of course. A Las Vegas brothel madam who has gained a measure of fame on the television talk-show circuit says she once threw Bogie out of her brothel and barred him for life because he was always drunk and had a habit of throwing lighted cigarette butts on the carpet. She didn't say when this occurred, but it would have been most uncharacteristic of him during the years I shared with him. But he was going through hell with his third wife, Mayo, even before I met him, and this might have happened during that period. Bogie was probably capable of such acts at that time.

His reputation as a drinker never diminished, but he cut down a good deal during the last ten years of his life. He never stopped drinking his "smashes," as he called them, of loudmouth, but he drank them in tall glasses, with plenty of soda and ice, and he would often make two or three of them last an entire evening. He always had a glass in hand, though, and the size of the drink made it appear that he was drinking much more than he actually was. Of course, sometimes he *did* drink as much as his reputation warranted, but not as often as people thought.

About halfway through our lunch, Bogie said, "We've got to get together, Pete. How can we call each other?"

"When I'm home, I can be reached before six in the evenings," I said.

"Is that when your old man gets home?"

"Usually, unless there's a card game or when he works overtime or on weekends when the fishing is good."

Bogie ordered another martini. "I can't drink too much," he said. "We're doing pickup shots to wrap the picture up. Is your house nearby?"

"Here in Burbank—on Roselli Street."

He asked the exact address and directions for getting there. Then he surprised me. "I'll go back over to the set and see if they're going to use me," he said. "I'll play sick or something and meet you at your place in about an hour. Is that okay with you?"

To this day, I don't know exactly how I reacted to that sudden turn of events. The only proof I have that I consented to his plan is that the next thing I remember is watching through the living-room window of my house as Bogie drove up in his Jaguar XK-120, parked in the driveway, walked briskly to my door, and rang the doorbell.

It was craziness. We were both married and had everything to lose by getting involved in an affair—and I knew (don't ask me how) that it wasn't going to be just a temporary fling. But here I was in my little house on a little street with barking dogs and nosy neighbors on the edge of Burbank, with Humphrey Bogart, whom the world could recognize from a mile away, standing on my front porch in broad daylight and ringing my doorbell. Worse yet, after we were caught during one of our trysts, Bogie began parking his car a block or two away and walking to the house; and during winter, he strode along in his damn trench coat, his damn snap-brim hat, and with that damn ever-present cigarette dangling from his famous face! I don't know whether we were amazingly lucky or whether Bogie was so obvious and out of place that none of the neighbors believed that the man they saw strolling down Roselli Street was really Humphrey Bogart.

It's difficult to explain our attraction for each other and the absurd risks we took to maintain our relationship. People will think what they want, regardless of what I write here, I suppose. But those who really knew Bogie understood that, down deep, he was a very moral man, and that he was prudish in some respects. The same can be said for me. Oh, I talk big, but I'm kind of a prude at heart. And Bogie aside, I had never strayed from the bounds of matrimony. I can only plead—for both of us—"temporary" insanity—for fifteen years.

Never did Bogie and I discuss or even consider the question of morality regarding our relationship. To us, there were no moral questions involved. It was inevitable. It was never a question of *should we* or *why* but *how:* how we could maintain our relationship; how we could overcome obstacles to it.

There were obstacles. And we didn't get away with our affair entirely. My husband caught us once—tipped off by the nosy wife of his neighborhood fishing buddy. It was a very weird experience.

Bogie and I had been to lunch together and had had too many smashes of loudmouth before rendezvousing at my place, where we continued to drink—among other things. When it came time for Bogie to leave, I judged that he had been drinking too much to drive, so I dragged him into a cold shower to sober him up. That was when my husband came bursting into the bathroom. And that sobered me up pretty fast, but it didn't seem to have the same effect on Bogie.

My husband began demanding to be told—at about fifty times the necessary decibel range—what the hell was going on. Well, what was going on was all too apparent. I jumped from beneath the shower and slammed the shower door, leaving Bogie standing and sputtering in the cold spray. I could have explained my concern for a friend's drunken state and not wanting him to drink and drive; it was perfectly natural under such circumstances to administer black coffee and to prescribe a cold shower. But what was clear to my husband and didn't seem at all natural to him was the fact that I had been in the shower with Bogie and that we were both stark naked.

I don't know how much of it was booze or how much

of it was good acting on Bogie's part (afterward, whenever I asked him about the episode, he would only laugh and say that he was smashed), but Bogie was absolutely incensed and on the offensive. The offensive! I couldn't believe it.

"Who the hell are you?" he was shouting at my husband. "What right do you have invading our privacy? Who *is* this son of a bitch, Pete? See here, you son of a bitch, I'll teach you to break into a lady's bathroom! Goddamn it, Pete, let me out of this fucking shower! We're not dealing with a gentleman here, Pete! See here, you son of a bitch. . . ."

They were both shouting at the same time, and it seemed to last for hours and hours, but it probably didn't go on for more than a minute or so. It must have been a bizarre sight from my husband's point of view: me bare-ass naked, dripping wet, arched against the shower door with my foot braced against the toilet bowl for leverage; Bogie still beneath the cold shower, bumping and thumping and banging against the door in an effort to get out and stopping every few seconds to shake a fist and to shout—in a voice loud enough to inform the entire neighborhood—that my husband was not a gentleman.

The end was as abrupt as the beginning. Apparently overwhelmed by the absurdity of it all, my husband stomped from the bathroom, through the house, and out the front door, slamming it with such force that it sounded like a cannon had gone off in the neighborhood. Then all was quiet, except for a few afterthoughts from Bogie, who was fumbling with the faucets in an effort to turn off the cold water and mumbling about how he would have "taught that son of a bitch some manners" if he could have gotten his hands on him.

I finally let Bogie out of the shower and tried to get him out of the place fast. It wasn't easy. He didn't want to leave me alone; he was concerned that my husband would return in a fit of rage. I knew my husband wasn't dangerous; he was a gentle man, dispassionate, even, and certainly not violent. But I was worried that he might indeed return with my nosy neighbor as a witness to my infidelity—grounds for divorce that, considering Bogie's stardom, would most certainly have made headlines in every newspaper in the country. But I had a hell of a time getting that across to Bogie, and I had to help him dress and shove him out of the house— though only after he made me swear at least half a dozen times that I'd call him at home if there was any trouble.

Needless to say, the event marked the end of my marriage, but it wasn't the cause of its dissolution, just a contributing factor. It would have been only a matter of time before we parted company, anyway. My husband had been good to me, and he was a very sweet guy —he could have ruined Bogie's career and didn't. I have to face the fact that *I* was the bitch, but as the old song goes, he only wanted a buddy, not a sweetheart, and that's not what I had in mind when I married him. Ironically, he was drafted before we could file for divorce, so we remained married in name only for the duration of World War II; but we divorced afterward.

My affair with Bogie continued without interruption.

Bogie and Me

We had been lucky that it was my husband and not Bogie's wife, Mayo, who caught us. Had it been Mayo, there would have been worldwide headlines, and probably bloody ones.

4

Mayo

The lowest point in Bogie's personal life had to be his seven-year marriage to Mayo Methot, his third wife and the one to whom he was married when I met him. It was as sad a love story as that of Scott and Zelda Fitzgerald, and far more spectacular. Bogie and Mayo were notorious for their knockdown, drag-out fights. I was one of many in town who thought that if they didn't divorce, one of them would eventually die at the drunken hands of the other.

Like Bogart's previous two wives, Mayo had been a Broadway actress. And when she received well-deserved acclaim in two hit Broadway plays (playing opposite George M. Cohan in one of them), she was called to Hollywood. Mayo met Bogie in 1937 and married him the following year. She was thirty-five then— three years younger than Bogie—in a town that worshipped youth, and her career was languishing. She had fallen in with the drinking crowd and was putting on weight because of it; in short, when she promised Bogie that she'd sacrifice her career for marriage, it wasn't much of a sacrifice. But the promise was important to him.

Bogie's marriage to actress Mary Philips had lasted nine years, but it had all but ended when Mary insisted on continuing her Broadway career at a time when Bogie had decided at last to stay in motion pictures and Hollywood. Their career separations were lengthy, and when Mary once returned unannounced to the West Coast from New York and found that Mayo had moved in with Bogie in their Garden of Allah bungalow, she divorced him. Bogie believed their divorce had been precipitated by their conflicting careers. He didn't want to get into the same situation with Mayo; instead, he got into a worse one.

When it came to choosing wives, Bogie seemed to be governed by an unfailing sense of indirection and a Puritan heart. His biographers have noted that he had affairs with each of his women before marrying them—and usually while he was still married to the previous one—and that his apparent need to do the right and honorable thing by them was, or seemed to be, a factor in his many trips to the altar. I think there's some truth in these observations. Bogie used to call himself a turn-of-the-century man (because he was born December 25, 1899), and he was a Victorian in many ways. This was most often evidenced by seemingly insignificant personal habits and attitudes. It often appeared to me that whatever was frowned upon by Victorian society was frowned upon by Bogie, too. But, as with most of us, he was often philosophically inconsistent: language and behavior that would have been unthinkable to Victorian society might be perfectly acceptable to Bogie.

As is customary in the entertainment industry,

among others, Bogie often used the foulest language in his everyday vocabulary; but he found the word *shit* repugnant. He would have been horrified by today's youth, who, in seeking to bring order to their lives, talk about "getting their shit together." Well, Bogie might have called them fucking assholes for using such language.

Victorian mores seemed to be his frame of reference regarding what he judged to be right conduct, and that was where his spirit dwelled even if his flesh was sometimes weak. Many of Bogie's idiosyncracies seem quite logical from this point of view; I think it was characteristic of him to feel somewhat obligated to wed those he bedded. His flaw, then, if one can call it that, lay in being attracted to and bedding women who, for one reason or another, were incapable of offering the stability he needed. And in this, there's no better example than Mayo Methot.

Mayo was everything Bogie loved: intelligent, vivacious, independent, witty, charming, and, above all, a character. Bogie loved characters—had a weakness for them—and Mayo, early on and when sober, was a delightful one. They first met at the home of a mutual writer-friend while Bogie's second wife, Mary, was in New York. Much to the chagrin of the writer and his wife, Mayo and Bogie continued using their home as a trysting place until Mayo finally moved in with Bogie. They married not long after Bogie's divorce became final.

In his biography *Humphrey Bogart,* author Nathaniel Benchley intimates that Bogie didn't love any of his first three wives. Perhaps he said this out of deference to Betty (Lauren Bacall), Bogie's last wife and the one to whom Benchley dedicated the biography. Benchley was also one of the biographers who believed that Bogie married only to assuage his conscience; Betty, he says, was the exception. In my opinion, this is pure crap. The inference one gets from Mr. Benchley's judgment is that Bogie was a spineless, mindless simpleton who was bullied into marriage by three women he didn't even love. That's absurd.

Bogie didn't talk to me at all about his first wife, actress Helen Menken, to whom he was married less than a year. But I know he had loved Mary Philips and adored Mayo Methot. To suggest otherwise is, at best, a treacherous assumption—one that Mr. Benchley wouldn't have dared make while Bogie was still alive. No, Bogie loved Mayo Methot, but the sad truth is that Mayo's mental health deteriorated badly in the first few years of their marriage, and in the end, she was nothing at all like the woman he married in 1938. Ironically, all the little idiosyncracies that had made Mayo the character in whom Bogie found nothing but delight were, in the end, exaggerated grotesquely; Bogie became the helpless victim of the very things that had attracted him to Mayo.

Bogie was a man of simple tastes and pleasures. Give him a pleasant house for shelter, an acting role that challenged his ability, a few changes of clothing—nothing fancy—a few smashes of loudmouth, a plate of ham and eggs, a good argument at a lively party, and a mate that didn't bore him, and he was a happy man. The woman he first saw in Mayo Methot was exactly what he was looking for. She was a two-fisted drinker who could hold her liquor; a gregarious party-goer; a fun-loving, sharp-tongued wit who liked nothing better than stimulating conversation; and, like Bogie, she hated pretentiousness and phonies. Her tastes, too, were simple, although I don't know whether she shared Bogie's dread of "going Hollywood." In his view, succumbing to the lust for fame, power, and money at any cost, along with the big cars and bigger mansions in Beverly Hills and all the other affectations, had "infected" and ruined many good actors. For years, Bogie refused to consider moving to Beverly Hills, seeing it as the irreversible first step to "going Hollywood."

So Mayo was a woman after Bogie's own heart. They married, bought a house on Horn Avenue in the Hollywood hills above the Sunset Strip, and settled in. They might have lived happily ever after—there was little chance of the boredom Bogie dreaded creeping into their marriage. But well into their second or third year, Bogie discovered that Mayo had a crazy streak as well as a penchant for physical violence that was made worse by alcohol. The change in her wasn't abrupt; that was one of the problems. Mayo's metamorphosis was so gradual that Bogie was trapped in her crazy web before he even realized it was developing.

It began innocently enough. Mayo was a strong-willed and tough little dame. She would lash out with her fists when she was provoked, and Bogie nicknamed her Sluggy. He even renamed his motor launch *Sluggy* after her, and their house on Horn Avenue he called Sluggy Hollow. She was totally unpredictable, and Bogie loved that; she worshipped him and was jealous of him, and Bogie thought that was cute; she was easily provoked into argument, which was Bogie's favorite pastime; she matched him drink for drink (and then some), and Bogie admired her for that; and she had a fiery nature, and that totally captivated him.

There was a strange and unfortunate chemistry between them. They thrived on the adversity of their union. In those first few years, they drank and argued and wrestled and made love, which called for another round of drinking and arguing and wrestling and lovemaking. But then another streak emerged in Mayo; no doubt it had always been just beneath the surface, for there had been signs of it in her earlier behavior. A sadistic and perhaps masochistic pattern emerged, and their playful little wrestling tussles began getting more violent, until her attacks became so vicious that it took all Bogie's strength to ward them off. Soon he was having to slug her to protect himself and to gain a semblance of order.

Once the line had been crossed where violence became, if not acceptable, then at least habitual, their fights grew irrational and spectacular, and even began erupting in public. By this time, Mayo was beyond using just her fists; she used bottles, bookends, vases—anything at hand. And more than once directors had to film Bogie from unusual angles to hide black eyes and cuts inflicted by Mayo that makeup couldn't cover. Once she stabbed him in the back with a knife.

Mayo's jealous nature turned irrational, too. She grew increasingly suspicious of Bogie—and she had no cause at the time—accusing him of having affairs with the leading ladies in his films. She began calling him at the studio and disrupting his concentration. Occasionally she'd show up at the set in a jealous rage, disrupting everything. When she was finally barred from the lot, she sometimes waited for hours outside the studio, spying to see whom Bogie left with. She called their friends constantly, trying to catch him in an affair or attempting to track him down when she didn't know exactly where he was. Her jealousy may have reached its zenith during the filming of *Casablanca,* in which Bogie was cast as a lover for the first time in his career, opposite Ingrid Bergman. Mayo was convinced that Bogie and Bergman were having an affair. In truth, they hardly knew one another. Bergman had been loaned to Warner Brothers by David O. Selznick to do just one picture, and though she and Bogie respected each other's work, they didn't even become friends, let alone lovers.

I entered the scene at about this time, and I honestly don't believe that Bogie had been seeing anyone before me. Perhaps he'd begun looking around for female companionship because his life with Mayo had become intolerable for him. I don't know; we never discussed such things. I know only that Bogie wasn't a loner, and that if his marriage had all but officially ended at that point, he had to have someone to love. It had happened toward the end of each of his marriages. But at that time, his marriage to Mayo was by no means at an end; she wouldn't let him go.

It ultimately dawned on Bogie that Mayo was far more troubled than he had realized. It weighed on him heavily. He hadn't been blameless; he wasn't just the victim of a bad marriage. There was something in him that made him needle people, provoke them; and his wife had been awfully sensitive to such provocation. Bogie wasn't violence-prone—far from it. He had never been violent with his women before or after Mayo, to my knowledge. He was really a gentle and sensitive person. But the chemistry between Mayo and him al-

tered *his* behavior as well. It brought out the worst in
him, as though Mayo somehow aroused in him uncivilized, primitive, predatory instincts that—in Bogie, at
least—lay very near the surface. They were fatally attracted to one another.

Bogie confided to me that he thought Mayo had become, in his words, "a schizo"; it was obvious to him
that she was an alcoholic as well. And when he realized
that she was incorrigible, he knew that a continuation
of their relationship would be disastrous. At the time
that I had begun seeing him, he had separated from
Mayo numerous times, but their separations had lasted
only two or three days at a time. Usually Bogie was
intimidated or frightened back to her by her threats of
suicide. Bogie told me that she had attempted suicide
twice. He was terrified that she might actually kill herself, that his leaving her might precipitate it—that he
might, in effect, be responsible for her death.

This is the mess I got myself into. At the time, I didn't
know how bad the situation was. I had heard of the
"battling Bogarts," as everyone in the business had, but
it was a while before I learned from Bogie what I've
related here. I met Mayo on two occasions in my first
couple of years with Bogie, and that was two times too
many. I'm not easily intimidated by people, but I went
out of my way to avoid Mayo Methot. My relationship
with Bogie was enough of a gamble with his career at
stake, but if Mayo had learned of it, there would have
been more at stake than merely his career.

5

Curtain

With my marriage on the rocks and my husband away in the service, I continued meeting Bogie at my place in Burbank. Often he'd spend the night, usually leaving for the studio at around five in the morning—these were times when he had separated briefly from Mayo or when she had driven him from the house with a barrage of bottles, dishes, pots and pans, and drunken screams.

My Burbank house became his refuge when he was drunk. He was much more cautious when sober and avoided coming directly to my place from his for fear that Mayo might follow him. But there were countless times when my doorbell would ring in the wee hours of the morning and I'd find Bogie standing on my porch, drunk and sometimes only half-clothed, having fled from Mayo in whatever state of dress he was in when the battle turned against him. Such visits were usually precipitated by Bogie's attempts at serious discussion with her. They'd sit down to talk rationally about their incompatibility and to consider the possibility of divorce; they'd usually have a few drinks. Then they'd have a few more drinks and a few more until their discussion turned to argument, which more often than not degenerated into warfare. But even when they avoided armed conflict, Mayo would often force a marathon argument, refusing to let Bogie sleep, and he'd have to flee in order to get a few hour's sleep before having to report to the studio that morning.

So he spent a good many nights at my place and some at the studio, where he'd sleep on his dressing-room couch. On one occasion, he had left Mayo in the middle of the night and was so drunk that rather than flopping on his couch at the studio, he rode around the lot on his studio bicycle, dressed only in his pajamas. The studio guards finally had to call Jack Warner because they couldn't talk Bogie off the bicycle and he was driving it so recklessly that they were afraid he'd seriously injure himself.

More often than not, though, he came to my Burbank house. These were unsettling times, to say the least, and they began taking their toll on me. At first, I didn't know how to handle Bogie when he'd wake me in the middle of the night. Inevitably he'd talk me into having a little smash of loudmouth with him, and we'd talk and drink and both get drunk—which didn't help him at all. I think drinking with him helped anesthetize my fear that Mayo might come crashing through the door with an ax or something. But I soon learned to appeal to his sense of professional pride and his need to be clear-headed before the camera. That always worked when he was shooting a picture. Bogie took his work very seriously, and so I was able to pump coffee into him instead of loudmouth, and often we'd stay up, talking, until it was time for him to report to the studio. This tack didn't work when he wasn't on a picture, but he was seldom between pictures for very long.

We talked often at such times about getting married once we got our divorces. Bogie always said that we'd make a perfect couple because we were so much alike, and I naturally agreed with him. I was thrilled at the prospect at first, but later I began having misgivings. I didn't tell Bogie this, of course; I wasn't really sure myself.

As Bogie's relationship with Mayo grew ever worse and divorce proceedings were finally in the offing, Bogie began needling me and pressuring me about my getting a divorce. I felt trapped and more than a little irritated with him. My husband hadn't filed, thinking, perhaps, that we could patch things up after the war— although I was absolutely sure we couldn't. I believe he thought my "infatuation" with Bogie would end and that I'd settle into the hausfrau routine he expected of me. I couldn't. There had to be more to marriage than his version of it, I thought, and although he loved me in his fashion, a sister or even his mother could have replaced me in his household. Still, he didn't file for divorce, and I couldn't, either. I could hardly claim mental cruelty when he wasn't even home to be mentally cruel. Nor could I file claiming that *I* was unfaithful to *him*. I was, as Bogie often lamented, "locked into" the marriage for the duration, and I was very confused about my future.

Finally, just before Bogie's own divorce proceedings began and he was talking as though the divorce were already final, he began taking issue with me in a way that I thought was irrational under the circumstances.

"What the hell are you waiting for, Pete?" he'd say. "If you file now, our divorces will become final at about the same time, and we can get married."

It was then that I told him of the misgivings I'd been having about marrying him. I was reluctant even to broach the subject; I wasn't at all sure, and the timing was bad, but he was bugging hell out of me. I gave it to him straight, the way Bogie always wanted it. I told him that I loved him, but that our getting married might be the worst idea he had had since his decisions to marry his three previous wives. I told him he had lousy taste in wives, that he chose them as a fighter would choose sparring partners. I told him that he drank too much and that I drank too much when I was with him, and that really worried me. I told him that maybe our fiery natures were too combustible for the restraints of marriage, and that he had characteristics that I tolerated—and occasionally delighted in—as a friend, but that I wasn't sure I could live with, such as his always having to needle people to the brink of fight or flight. I told him other things, too, but that was the substance of it.

We were sitting at my kitchen table having a drink when I gave my little speech. I finished and sat back, expecting him to give me both barrels. Instead, he fell silent for a long time, smoking and contemplating his drink. Finally he said, "Hell, Pete, maybe you're right. I have botched three marriages, and they were all good women. Damn good women. But, Pete, I really love you—I mean the kind of love that doesn't die. You're the only woman in my life."

"You loved the others, too," I said.

"Yes. I still do, in a way. But, Christ, I must have learned *something* from my past mistakes. Maybe you're right about me. I certainly was to blame for all three failures, but maybe I could change. Hell, I *could* change."

"That's some way to launch a marriage," I said, "marrying and then trying to be someone else afterward."

"I gotta think about this," Bogie said. "You're so goddamned dispassionately logical about all this that it frightens me!"

"Me, too," I said.

Several months later, when the divorce papers were about to be filed, I told Bogie I thought it best for us to break off our relationship until his divorce was over and I had arranged for mine. That way, I told him, there would be no chance of me being named as a correspondent in his divorce proceedings. Besides, I was a nervous wreck by then, caught between Bogie and Mayo—and who knew what she might do?—and hiding from the studio brass, hiding from the public, drinking too much with Bogie, getting little sleep, and being pressured by Bogie at every turn to get a divorce. It was getting so that we were beginning to argue as much as he and Mayo had, and that was the last thing that he or I needed.

Bogie agreed in principle to break off our relationship temporarily, but within a few days, he was talking about our getting together again. "What the hell good does our not seeing each other do?" he kept saying. "I told you that I love you, Pete, no matter what. But why this torture? What is not seeing each other for months going to accomplish? Mayo's in Reno for the divorce.

Christ! When she was here, we were together. Now she's in another state, and we're apart. Does that make any sense at all?"

He raised the subject twice at the studio, but in such dispassionate surroundings that reason prevailed. Bogie was a man of his word, though. He didn't come to the house again; he had made an agreement, and he would keep it. But he wanted to renegotiate the agreement and kept calling me—often waking me in the middle of the night—to discuss it. There was a time or two when I was sorely tempted to forget about the damn logical agreement, for he was very lonely and drinking too much, and I was lying awake nights worrying about him. But to have begun seeing him again would have landed us both neck deep in problems, so I firmly resolved not to give in. I finally began taking my phone off the hook at night.

I saw very little of Bogie even at the studio during the next few months. I told Gordon Bau that I was booked solid and couldn't get away to work with Bogie on his picture—this was a few months after the rib we had staged for Gordon. Then Bogie finally went back East, and I began reading in the trades that he was escorting a young actress named Lauren Bacall around New York (he had just completed *To Have and Have Not* with her). I didn't give it much thought at the time. It could be a publicity gimmick. His divorce wasn't final yet. Who could believe the columnists, anyway?

As the date of Bogie's divorce decree drew near, I wondered how I'd react when he got in touch with me again. He would be free from Mayo and her threats, and I doubted whether I could be so firm in my resolve not to see him again before I got my own marriage problems straightened out. Even with Mayo gone it would be dangerous for him to start seeing me; I was still married. But it was soon evident that I had been wasting my time worrying.

Twelve days after Bogie's divorce became final, the newspapers announced that he had married Bacall on Louis Bromfield's farm in Ohio.

I was furious at first, then I cried for several days at the shock of the news. I took it so hard, in fact, that my dearest friend, Annie Locker, came and stayed with me at my Burbank house for a few days and helped me through my emotional squalls. Annie was my only confidante (Annie Sheridan was by then living in Mexico, I believe), and she had known about my affair with Bogie from its beginning. So I naturally turned to her, and of course she took my side and agreed that I had been betrayed. We both raged against Bacall, whom we viewed as an opportunistic Jane-come-lately. Perhaps irrationally, neither of us held Bogie accountable for the action. And we both lamented that I had been so damned logical and so damned overprotective of Bogie's image that I had scratched myself from the race —a race that I hadn't known was being run—while some unknown late entry slithered across the finish line. I was sick, and I hated myself for what I'd done. Now, thanks to me and my damned dispassionate reasoning, it was over.

At least I thought it was over.

Part Two

6

Curtain Call

I was still at home one morning in August 1945, just a week or so before V-J Day, as I recall, when the phone rang. It was Bogie. It had been about three months since he had married Betty Bacall, and I hadn't seen him since. From the noise in the background, I judged that he was calling from one of the phones on a sound stage.

"Pete?" he said. "Are you accepting calls from Humphrey Bogart?"

"Humphrey *who?*" I said. It was a running joke of ours; he used to call me and say, "This is Bogie," as though I couldn't recognize that distinctive voice of his, so I'd say, "Bogie who?"

"Humphrey Bogart," he said. "Big movie star. Wants to take you to lunch. Are you free?"

"I haven't even had breakfast yet," I said.

"Oh, I forgot about you late-sleeping civilians. Let's make it brunch, then. I've got some business to talk to you about."

"Okay, I guess so," I said. "Where do you want to meet?"

"How about the Smoke House, say in about fifteen or twenty minutes?"

"Fifteen minutes? I haven't even put my face on yet, and the one I'm wearing looks like something an archeologist dug up."

Bogie laughed. "Out late with the boys again, huh?"

"I'm trying not to remember."

"That bad, huh? Well, I'd have called you sooner, but we're just breaking for lunch. C'mon. I'll even treat you to a Bloody Mary . . . about half an hour?"

"That's the best offer I've had all morning—I think. But make it forty-five minutes. I've got a major overhaul to do on this mug of mine."

"Okay, I'll arrange it."

Bogie was sitting in one of the booths across from the bar when I arrived. He looked terrific, better than he had in a long time. The all-night drinking and fighting bouts he had gotten into with Mayo had taken their toll on him, and the strain had shown. But now he looked relaxed, younger. There was a Bloody Mary on the table, waiting for me. I hadn't been in the Smoke House for a while, and meeting Bogie there again naturally brought back memories of our first meeting three years earlier. I felt like saying something about returning to the scene of the crime, but I didn't.

For one of the few times in my adult life, I felt awkward. I didn't really know how to greet him or what to say, but he took care of that. He jumped to his feet, grabbed me, and gave me a big kiss. It had only been about five months since I had last seen him, which had been a couple of months before he married Bacall, but it seemed ages. I didn't take the meeting lightly, but I tried to keep it light—at first. "So," I said, "what's new with you?"

"Yeah, well, I did it again, Pete."

"Un-huh. I read it in the paper."

"I'd have called you and told you first, but you wouldn't have answered my call anyway."

"Some guys can't pass up a saloon," I said. "With you it's saloons and altars."

"You're still a sassy li'l bitch, aren't you?"

"I'm surprised you remember," I said. "Just getting the first needle in before you do. I'm a little rusty at it —haven't had anyone to practice with."

I had missed exchanging barbs with Bogie, but I didn't realize how much until that moment. I was getting something out of my system, too. It was probably because I still loved him and felt that I shouldn't. Anyway, I was feeling really bitchy and finding emotional release in needling him just then, and I decided to stick him with another one. "From the photographs I've seen of Bacall," I said, "you're safe. She's not carrying enough weight to pack a big punch."

Bogie was silent for a moment, then said, "Let's keep Betty out of this."

"It's a little late for that!" I said. "What is it with you? We stop seeing each other—temporarily—and you go off and get married on me. And now you don't want to discuss it? You don't owe me *that* much? Every time you get a divorce, Bogie, you grab the nearest warm female body—like a drowning man—and you *marry* it!"

"Pete," Bogie said, "you know how I feel about you."

"I do now. I sure as hell do now, Bogie."

"It's not like you think."

"Not like I think," I said. "I'm sitting in Burbank, worrying about you, worrying whether we ought to get married because I didn't want you making another foolish mistake, wondering whether I could adjust and make you a good wife so that you could have a happy married life for the first time in your life, and you marry somebody who just *drifted* into your life! Who the hell is she, anyway? Comes into town, gets in her first movie —opposite the great Humphrey Bogart—and before the goddamn klieg lights on the set are cold, the great Bogart *marries* her. A total goddamned *stranger!*"

"Pete, I've told you a hundred times. You're the only woman in my life, and—"

I started to get up from the booth, but Bogie grabbed my hand and held me. "Pete, please. Hear me out."

"Bogie, you're making me crazy with this talk! Are you listening to what you're saying?"

"Goddamn it! I'm trying to level with you, trying to explain that it's not like you *think!* I know it sounds nuts, but it's not *anything* like you think—or like it looks. I told you I did it *again.* Okay, like you said—a drowning man. I didn't think about it. I got drunk and I got married and I don't even know how the hell it all happened! But now I'm locked in again, and I gotta figure a way out of it."

It was a non sequitur if I'd ever heard one. To put it quite simply—and it's an oversimplification—I was stunned.

"Out of your *marriage?*" I said.

"Yeah," Bogie said. "What the hell do you think I'm talking about?"

"I don't know *what* the hell you're talking about," I said. "Are you saying that you don't even love her?"

"I don't know what the hell I'm saying, Pete. She's a great broad, she really is, but . . ."

"But do you love her?"

"What the hell's love?" Bogie said.

"Don't toy with me, Bogie. I don't give a damn how you define love. I want to know if you love her, however you define it."

"All I know is that it's not like with you and me," he said. "Christ! I've really done it up good this time. An actress again, and an ambitious one. We haven't a damn thing in common, and she's young enough to be my daughter."

"*I'm* young enough to be your daughter," I said.

"In years, yeah. But that's not what I'm talking about. She really needs someone more her age. And she's an actress, and with this goddamned Hollywood and its Casanova leading men. I've really done it this time."

"So that's what's *really* worrying you. You're afraid she'll go running off with a Casanova and make you look like an ass!"

"No," Bogie said. "Well, the thought has crossed my mind, but that's not what I'm talking about. Look, I just want you to know that I still love you and that everything I've ever said in the past about us still stands. Please, Pete, don't hold this against me. I didn't do this to *you;* I did it to *me.*"

"And to Betty," I said.

"Christ! And to Betty, yes. I really screwed up. But I'll work it out, Pete. I've got to."

We sat in silence for a long while. I mentioned in an earlier chapter that Bogie had an unfailing sense of indirection when it came to choosing wives and that he seemed driven to the altar more from his moral imperative to do "the right thing" by the women in his life than from rational thought. It seemed to me that Bogie had suddenly found himself free and drunk, and so grabbed the nearest preacher and the latest entry and "did the right thing" to atone for his imagined sins.

Now we were back where we had begun: both locked into marriage and both hoping that our condition was temporary. As for Betty Bacall, I don't blame her for marrying Bogie. Who could blame her? But I didn't know her and I certainly wasn't going to shed any tears over the fact that after crossing the finish line in first place, she might be disqualified.

Admittedly, it's just my opinion, but Betty always struck me as being too chameleon-like: it seemed to me that before marriage she flashed all of the colors that Bogie found attractive; afterwards she showed her true ones, and Bogie didn't always seem too fond of the change. For example, her interest in the *Santana* and sailing delighted Bogie, for he spent—and wanted to spend—every spare moment sailing. But Betty's interest in going to sea with Bogie declined after he slipped a ring on the third finger of her left hand. Her dwindling interest in the *Santana* left clear sailing for me, but it reinforced Bogie's initial belief that he and Betty had few common interests.

Another problem was Bogie's liking for down-to-earth women, women who had both feet on the ground. But it seemed to Bogie that they were no sooner married when Betty's feet were dancing up the rungs of the social ladder. He often lamented that she had a penchant for putting on airs and that he had to pierce her ego occasionally. I don't know if Bogie was kidding when he told me, "When we first met, she talked like a goddamn dead-end kid—all deze, dem, and doze. I had to teach her *English,* for God's sake, and before I knew it she was trying to go high-hat on me with her *society* stuff!"

I was nonplussed. Finally Bogie motioned toward my drink. "If that's too watery, I'll order you another," he said. "I had it put out early to discourage anyone from joining me before you got here."

I sipped the drink. "It's fine," I said, "but if this doesn't revive me, haul me over to Forest Lawn Mortuary, will you?"

Bogie laughed, obviously relieved to change the subject. "You're gonna live, ol' girl," he said. "Actually, you look pretty good. The way you talked on the phone, I expected you to be carried in here on a stretcher."

"Not a stretcher, a wheelchair," I said. "I couldn't get the damn thing up the steps, so I parked it outside."

By this time Bogie wasn't even listening, and I was just chattering to keep my mind off what he had told me. Humor can be sanity restoring, and I sure as hell needed that at the moment.

"So where the hell have you been?" Bogie asked. "Gordon keeps telling me that you're busy all the time. You can't be *that* busy."

I shrugged and said nothing. I had turned down some work at Warner Brothers, but not much. I had avoided going anywhere near Bogie, having convinced myself that it was the proper thing to do under the circumstances. But, in truth, I was afraid to be around him. I wasn't sure how I'd react, and while being around him again might have been a good self-disciplinary trial for building character, I didn't want the pain that would go with it.

"Listen, Pete, how the hell can you go off and just leave me at the mercy of all those fags? I mean, they're prancing in and fluffing up my muff between every goddamn take! What the hell kind of a way is that to treat a friend?"

"You haven't got any fags fluffing up your muff," I said.

"How the hell do you know? You haven't even been around."

"Because I know the people in makeup over here, and they're not fags."

"Well, they *could* be fags, for all I know. Anyway, they're doing a lousy job."

He had come directly over from the set and was still in makeup and toupee. "That toup looks fine to me," I said.

"Yeah? Well, you don't have to wear it. It doesn't feel right. It's bothersome, Pete. Feels like I'm wearing a goddamn helmet all the time. Must be they put it on too tight or something. I don't know. But it breaks my concentration."

We discussed his toupee and the fitting of it for a minute or so, but Bogie suddenly changed the subject by throwing me a haymaker of a question. I could say that his question surprised me, but I'm not really sure that it did. That may sound strange, but the fact is that everything about our relationship always seemed rehearsed. It wasn't *déjà vu*. I didn't get the feeling or mental picture that I had had the same experience before. It was as though I had long ago memorized and subsequently forgotten the script of our relationship, so that everything that occurred seemed comfortable and, if not destined, not altogether unfamiliar. It was as

though our roles had been rehearsed but never played
out until the moment we cued one another. Then the
scenes unfolded, because that was the way they were
written, and we were merely following the script. I'm
not implying anything supernatural here nor offering
this as a rationalization for my—our—behavior. It's just
the way it was.

Bogie's haymaker question was simple and direct,
which was his style. He asked it quietly and solemnly:
"Any chance that we might pick up where we left off,
Pete? I mean, not just with the damn muff. I can't get
you out of my mind."

I was surprised only by the speed of my answer.

"Of course," I said.

7

Other Arrangements

My professional relationship with Bogie had begun in 1944, shortly after the dressing-room rib I described in Chapter 1. A few days after that, I was called into Warner Brothers to view the screen test of the partial toupee I had designed for him. I sat next to Bogie in the screening room; Gordon Bau took a seat behind us. I was more than a little nervous, afraid that Bogie might not like what he saw on the screen; this was business, and Bogie never compromised on anything having to do with his profession. If he didn't like what I had done with his hair, the fact that we were lovers wouldn't mean a thing.

As Bogie watched the screen, he chewed gum so fast and hard that I was sure it was a sign I had failed. He didn't take his eyes off the screen once, and he didn't utter a word during the screening. But when the lights went up—and I fully expected to be tossed out of the screening room on my ass—he turned to me, grinning and tugging at his right earlobe (which, I had learned, was his habit, usually in moments of bemused thought, and not a screen affectation), and said, "Not bad, ol' girl. Not bad at all." Then he turned to Gordon Bau, saying, "Make a deal with Pete," then back to me. "But no hairstylist stuff," he said. "From now on, you're my executive secretary and adviser."

I didn't understand what he was getting at. It hadn't occurred to me that he didn't want someone on the lot who would be known as "the tough guy's hairdresser" —though in later years, he often told people that I was his hairstylist. So I said, "I don't take dictation, and my typing stinks."

"Who said anything about typing? I said *executive,* ol' girl, executive secretary." Then he nudged me and winked.

Our little plan didn't turn out as well as we had hoped. The Warner Brothers makeup department couldn't fault the job I had done on Bogie, but that didn't mean they were happy at the prospect of my working with him; in fact, I'm sure they looked upon the arrangement as setting an undesirable precedent. If word got around that Bogie had his own hairstylist, independent of the makeup department, other stars might demand the same treatment. So even after Gordon Bau made a deal with me, there was a lot of stalling on the part of Warner Brothers. I was given enough work to appease Bogie for a while but not enough to warrant being called Bogie's personal hairstylist.

I was put on payroll for the film *Conflict,* which was released in 1945, but that picture was followed by two others before I was put back on payroll for *Dead Reckoning.* I don't know whether I refused to work on *The Big Sleep,* which Bogie did with Bacall, or whether I just wasn't offered the picture—probably the latter. I don't recall even touching Bogie's hair for *Conflict,* even though I was on payroll, so I believe *Dead Reckoning* was the first film I actually worked on. Bogie did two other films after that, *Dark Passage* and *Always Together,* before I was again assigned to work with him. (A third film, *The Two Mrs.Carrolls,* was released at this time, too, but it was a delayed release; the picture had been completed nearly two years earlier.) I think I had another film commitment during the filming of *Always Together* but didn't get a call on it, and Bogie was mad about that.

The filming of *The Treasure of the Sierra Madre* was a turning point in our professional association. I was put on payroll for that one and did the partial toupees he used in the film, but someone in the makeup department was sent to Mexico to fit them, and I remained in Hollywood.

When Bogie returned from location shooting in Mexico on *Sierra Madre,* his hair was a mess; it was falling out not just in strands but in patches. In his biography, Nathaniel Benchley claims that Bogie was taking hormone shots at the time. I know nothing about this; Bogie used to take a lot of vitamin-B shots for his general health and to counter the effects of too much loudmouth, but he never mentioned taking hormones. Benchley might be right, though; this would certainly account for his sudden loss of hair. Anyway, after *Sierra Madre,* Bogie had need of a full frontal toupee. Prior to this, he hadn't had to use a toupee for personal appearances and the like, but no longer. By the way, Bogie's real head of hair can be seen in *Sierra Madre;* there's a delightful barber shop scene where Bogie's real hair is seen neatly cut and slicked back. As he leaves the barber shop, he dons his snap-brim hat, which comes down around his ears from having his hair shorn; it's a funny little bit, added by director John Huston and played nicely by Bogie.

It was also at about this time (1947) that Bogie got off the Warner Brothers assembly line by signing a fifteen-year contract. The pact required that he do only one picture a year, at about $300,000 per picture, and allowed him to free-lance. Before the new contract, Warners used to throw as many as three or four films at him a year. And if Bogie didn't like the films and refused to do any of them, Warners would suspend him without pay until he agreed to do another. Bogie was suspended at least a dozen times in the ten-year period before he renegotiated the contract.

The new contract gave Bogie the right to refuse without penalty films that he didn't think were good vehicles for him. Even so, the arrangement didn't give him the artistic fulfillment and control that he wanted, and toward this end, he was among the first of the film stars to go it alone by forming his own independent company, Santana Productions, which he named after his beloved 55-foot yawl *Santana.* Bogie made five films through Santana Productions, none of them very distinguished, but he was learning and had hopes and great plans for the company right up to the time of his death.

As it turned out, Bogie only did a half-dozen or so films under his new Warner Brothers contract. He had incurred Jack Warner's wrath by forming Santana Productions, and owing to television, the major studios were abandoning their costly contract-player system, so when Bogie wanted freedom from his contract to free-lance completely, Jack Warner was no doubt happy to oblige him. Bogie did only two films for Warner after *Sierra Madre;* they were *Key Largo* and *Chain Lightning.* I didn't work on either of them.

In early 1949, Bogie told me of his plans to leave Warner Brothers and to do more work with his own and other film companies. He would no longer be under Jack Warner's thumb, and he wanted me to work on all the Santana Productions films. He was reluctant to place himself in the hands of the makeup departments at the other production companies for whom he would work. "How do you figure we can work this, Pete?" he said. "Hell, I can't be haggling over contract details about hairstylists, and I might get stuck with somebody who doesn't know what the hell he's doing."

"Have me written into your personal agency contract," I told him. "That way whenever you're contracted for a picture, they'll have to call me."

So in 1949, Bogie arranged with Sam Jaffe, owner of The Jaffe Agency, to have me included in all contracts he signed with movie companies, and from that time on, I worked on all but four of Bogie's last eighteen pictures.

Assigning me to Bogie's agency contract accomplished far more than my introduction at Warner Brothers had. In the five years prior to this, we had had reason to be seen together, but owing to Warner Brothers' lack of cooperation, we avoided public places. After 1949, we not only frequented public places but traveled together, too. The day that Bogie arranged with Sam Jaffe for me to be included in his contracts, he took me to Romanoff's for a celebration lunch. It was the first time we had ever been to Romanoff's together, and

Bogie took advantage of the fact by pulling a rib on "Prince" Michael Romanoff.

Romanoff was the exception to Bogie's rule of not associating with or tolerating phonies. Romanoff had emigrated to New York from Europe. I don't know what his real name was, but he assumed the name Romanoff and the title of prince, claiming to be a member of the royal Russian family in exile. Under this guise, he charmed his way into New York society and soon gravitated to Hollywood, where he and a business partner opened a restaurant. He soon became a favorite with the film colony. When his restaurant ran into financial trouble, several actors (including Bogie) are said to have financed him, enabling him to buy out his partner and relocate the restaurant on fashionable Rodeo Drive in Beverly Hills, next door to the equally fashionable Beverly Wilshire Hotel.

Michael Romanoff was a consummate gentleman, highly civilized, intelligent, witty, and very charming. I think Bogie looked upon him as a fellow actor, or at least the practitioner of the biggest, longest-lasting, and most successful rib Bogie had ever seen. For an unknown immigrant to pose as a prince and charm his way into the highest social circles on both coasts was no mean feat, and Bogie was impressed.

On one hand, Bogie respected Romanoff for the big rib, and on the other, he respected him personally. Bogie told me he was convinced that Michael Romanoff was a far classier and more civilized man than a real Prince Romanoff would have been. And Bogie loved his restaurant; it was a home away from home, and he had lunch there every day he could when he was in town.

Bogie and Me

It's my feeling that Bogie liked the place because it was the house the rib built, as phony in its tinsel-town elegance as any movie set, and that, I'm sure, amused him. For another thing, he liked the place because he and Mike were good friends; they played chess together often, and Mike was frequently a dinner or cocktail-party guest at Bogie's home. Still, always the needler, Bogie usually referred to Mike affectionately as the phony prince. And Romanoff, who didn't take anything from anyone, needled Bogie right back.

So the first time Bogie took me to Romanoff's, Mike met us at the door. As usual, I didn't know that Bogie was going to pull a rib. Maybe he hadn't even planned to, but when he introduced me, he said, "Mike, this is Petée Gonzales, one of Mexico's most popular and accomplished actresses; Petée, this is Prince Michael Romanoff, of the imperial Romanoffs."

As Mike bowed and kissed my hand, I glanced at Bogie, who was grinning mischievously. I had been in Romanoff's a few times, but I was a Hollywood nobody, and so he had no reason to know who I was or to recognize me.

Taking my cue from Bogie, I asked in broken English whether Mike understood Spanish. He replied that to his regret, he didn't. He escorted us to Bogie's customary booth and sat down with us while we ordered lunch. I pretended to grope for English words whenever I couldn't conjure answers to Mike's questions fast enough. Bogie sat back, playing it straight and beaming; I felt like hitting him with my purse. Of course, it wasn't long before Bogie began directing the little drama he had gotten me into and answering questions for me, building the legend of Petée Gonzales.

"And what part of Spain are you from?" Romanoff asked.

"Mexico," Bogie said, "not Spain."

"Mexico?" Romanoff said, looking at me closely. "I've never seen a Mexican with blue eyes—and beautiful blue eyes, too, I might add."

"Well, there's a hell of a lot in this world you haven't seen, Mike," Bogie said.

"Blue ice?" I said.

Bogie looked over at me, and with an absolutely straight face, he rattled off something that sounded like *"Quanto pourto questa eyesetta costada, por favor."* It was, of course, except for the *por favor,* pure gibberish, but Mike took it for Spanish. I nearly fell out of the booth, and I couldn't keep from laughing, but Mike thought Bogie had said something in Spanish that amused me. I rattled off a non sequitur in Spanish back at Bogie, which would have translated to something like: Mexico gets dark at night and gets light again when the sun rises. It really didn't matter what I said; neither of them understood Spanish.

Bogie listened, then turned to Romanoff. "She says her father was Irish. That's where she gets the blue eyes. Her ol' man was a lot like you, Mike. Emigrated to Mexico from Ireland and passed himself off as a bullfighter because he always wanted to be one. Hadn't even seen a bull, I guess, but he had a lot of class and guts, and he became one of Mexico's finest matadors— the only Irish matador in the history of bullfighting. Christ, Mike, you must have heard of him: Ernesto Gonzales? That wasn't his real name, of course. I think Hemingway did a piece on him, didn't he, Petée? Didn't our Hemingway write about your father?"

"Oh, *sí,*" I said. "Very much write."

"I didn't know you spoke Spanish," Romanoff said to Bogie.

"I don't speak it well anymore," Bogie said. "One gets out of practice. But I understand it fluently."

"I'll be damned," Mike said.

Romanoff was very impressed. The portrait that Bogie had fashioned of my father was a man after Romanoff's own heart, so he warmed to me considerably. He kept getting up and greeting patrons as they entered, but in between greetings, he listened enthusiastically as Bogie built me into a stage and film legend. Finally, the phony prince, as Bogie called him, insisted on introducing me to a phony movie producer (Bogie's words; he really wasn't a phony). Romanoff talked to the producer at his table for a moment, no doubt telling him of my legend and of my famous father, Ernesto, then brought him to our table to make the introductions.

As they approached our booth, Bogie whispered to me, "When I give you the cue, you say—in flawless English—'This day will go down in infamy as one of our darkest.' "

"I don't speak flawless English," I said.

"Shhhh," he said.

Romanoff introduced us, and the producer asked how long I would be in town and the occasion of my visit. Bogie answered for me. "I've brought her up to put her in one of my own productions," he said. "She's going to be a very big star here, and I'm gonna sink plenty of dough into promoting her. Doesn't speak much English, but she's a smart broad. Learned the whole damn script phonetically in hours, and without a trace of accent. She's got a great ear. Give him the line you have after I order your father taken away to prison, Petée."

"*Sí*, Boogie," I said. Then, without accent, I said, "You're an impostor, Captain DeForest. This day will go down in infamy as the darkest in our history."

Bogie's face started to crack. Using his middle name in the line had surprised him. I looked away to keep from laughing. I was beginning to warm to the rib myself.

"That's wonderful," the producer said.

"Wonderful?" Bogie said, recovering. "It's goddamned sensational! The broad learned the whole goddamned hundred-and-forty-page script in a couple of hours. She's a goddamned *Einstein* in skirts!"

Finally the producer gave Bogie one of his cards, saying that he might find a part for me in one of his productions (producers are always saying this). Bogie gave him his card in return. "If you do," he said, "don't forget my commission."

The producer assumed that Bogie was serious and assured him that if he did use me, Bogie would indeed get the standard 10-percent commission.

After we left Romanoff's, Bogie was ecstatic. "You were great!" he said. "That was a wonderful rib."

It had been fun, but I wasn't quite so enthusiastic; I didn't relish having to speak broken English every time I went into Romanoff's—particularly if I went there without Bogie.

"Don't worry about it," Bogie said. "I've got another rib on the fire."

I assumed that Bogie would have me speaking perfect English the next time we went in, claiming to have taught me in a weekend. But that wasn't it.

We went into Romanoff's a couple of days later—Bogie couldn't wait any longer to pull his new rib. The "Prince" stumbled all over himself greeting me at the door as *his* Señorita Gonzales. Bogie stopped him cold.

"What the hell's the matter with you, Mike? You getting senile or something? This is my executive secretary, Verita Peterson. Christ! Can't you tell one broad from another? This is really *embarrassing!*"

Romanoff was momentarily shocked at his apparent *faux pas.* Then he studied my eyes for a moment and realized that he had once again been victimized by a Bogart rib. He was a very good sport, though, and we joked about it all through lunch.

Owing to my interest in the restaurant business, I got to be friends with Mike Romanoff. And when I opened my first restaurant years later, Mike—then in his eighties, I think, and retired—came to my opening. While all the other guests were out front, Mike had me giving him the cook's tour of the kitchen; he was like a child in a toy shop, and I had a hell of a time trying to get him out of the kitchen and back to the other guests. He often stopped in after that to have lunch or dinner and to give me advice; it was good advice, too, and welcome, since it was my first restaurant. It was kind of sad at the time, though. Mike had sold his place a few years earlier, and I could tell that he missed the business—even though any restaurateur of sound mind will tell you that it's one of the worst businesses in the world to get into. But, like printer's ink, I guess, it gets into your blood, where it exhilarates and poisons at the same time.

Other Arrangements

I told Mike that he could come in and run my place any time he wanted to. We spent many hours there, reminiscing about the past and about Bogie. Michael Romanoff is gone now, and I miss him.

8

Mr. Eisenhower and Mr. Zanuck

One of the first trips I took with Bogie in my capacity as hairstylist and secretary was to Denver, Colorado; I believe it was in late summer, 1951. Some Republicans were holding a fund-raising rally for Dwight Eisenhower, who was making his first bid for the presidency of the United States, against Adlai Stevenson. Darryl F. Zanuck, the majordomo of Twentieth Century-Fox, called Bogie one day to tell him he was organizing a party of actors and actresses to attend the rally; he asked if Bogie would like to join him.

Bogie was cynical about politics and politicians, but he was of the opinion that with rights come obligations (this was most evident in his work ethic and in the pride he took in his profession), and he felt that the least one could do for a country that offered so much was to participate in the democratic process that had established it and that would ensure its continuation. He wasn't much for group endeavors, though, or drum beating or flag waving. And as an individualist, he was likely to vote for the man rather than for the ticket. He was a registered Democrat, but he felt that Ike was a tougher and more pragmatic man than Stevenson, so he decided to vote for Eisenhower, while Betty Bacall remained in the Stevenson camp and didn't go to the Eisenhower fund-raiser.

Bogie told Zanuck that he wasn't a joiner, but that if all his expenses were paid—including those of his secretary—he'd attend. Zanuck agreed, and it was arranged.

We were picked up by a studio limousine and taken to Los Angeles International Airport, where we met Mr. Zanuck, Susan Hayward and her husband, Jess Barker, and a few others, including two publicity men. We boarded the plane; special seats had been sectioned off in the back for the Zanuck party. I sat down next to Bogie, and Zanuck took a seat opposite mine. Susan and Jess and other members of the party were seated across the aisle from us.

After a round of drinks while we were winging our way toward Denver, Bogie reclined his seat to take his customary in-flight nap. Zanuck, whom I'd just met for the first time, kept up a running conversation with me and was getting awfully familiar; it seemed to me that he was getting *too* familiar, but I dismissed the idea as ridiculous. Soon he decided to take a nap too. He got out his traveling slippers and eyeshade mask and put them on, settling back in his seat. A few minutes passed; I was looking out the window when I felt something on my foot. I looked down to discover that the big movie mogul was playing footsie with me. I couldn't believe it. There he was, stretched back as though sleeping, eyeshades on, and he was groping for me with his slippered foot! I pulled my feet back and looked around to see if anyone had seen the action. Jess Barker, who had the aisle seat across from me, was smiling. He leaned toward me and whispered, "You'd better watch him, Pete. He's got his eye on you."

"He's going to have two black eyes on me if he doesn't watch his manners," I said aloud.

Jess laughed, and I kept track of Zanuck's vagabond feet throughout the rest of the flight. I couldn't believe that one of the biggest movers and shakers in the movie industry would put such a juvenile move on me, but I learned before the trip was over that Mr. Z wasn't easily discouraged.

We were met at the Denver airport with a fleet of limousines and were taken to the hotel where the Zanuck party was to stay. Bogie and I went up to his suite, where I called room service and ordered a bottle of Scotch, two of soda, glasses and ice. That was always the first order of business whenever Bogie checked into a hotel. Then I got his toupees out, brushed them and placed them on blocks before putting them in the closet out of sight in case someone should happen to drop in.

When the Scotch arrived, we had a drink; then Bogie decided to shower and dress. We were to attend a black-tie dinner party, thrown for Ike at a private residence, then go to an auditorium where Ike was giving a campaign speech. While Bogie was showering, I went to my suite to unpack and do the same. There I found an enormous bouquet of flowers and a bowl of fruit; the attached card read: "Thinking of you. We can have fun, if you're willing."

It was signed "Mr. Z," and it irritated me. As are most women, I've always been sensitive about being taken for granted and being chased as just another skirt. In any business, there's always some big monkey who gets a couple of drinks under his belt and thinks that women should fall all over him because of his lofty position. They mean nothing personal by it, of course, and that's exactly the problem.

I took a shower to cool down, and just as I was finished dressing, the phone rang. Sure enough, it was Zanuck.

"Hello, doll," he said. "How about coming up to my suite for a glass of champagne before we leave—just the two of us?"

I had regained my cool. I refused him politely. "I've got too much to do for Mr. Bogart," I said. "People to contact, letters—that sort of thing." I thanked him for the fruit and flowers.

"Oh, that's nothing," he said. "You get rid of that Bogart and come up to my suite and I'll see that you have more than just flowers."

I was getting pissed at him again. "I'll bet you would," I said.

"Well, maybe later," he said. "I'll call you."

Mr. Zanuck was not easily brushed. I went down to Bogie's suite, still fuming. He was just putting on his shirt and tie when I arrived; he opened the door, took one look at me as I breezed by him, and said, "What the hell's eating you?"

"It's that damn Zanuck," I said. "My damn room's full of flowers and fruit from him, then he's on the phone whispering his version of sweet nothings!"

"Aw, cool down and fix us a smash," Bogie said, tying his tie before the mirror. "That'll calm you down. What the hell you taking this so seriously for, anyway?"

I mixed us a drink, then began applying Bogie's toupee, muttering to myself about footsie, flowers, and fruit. "The big three *f*s," I said.

Bogie was amused. "Four," he said, "if you include phone—well, phonetically speaking, of course."

"Very funny," I said. "Well, I've got another *f* for him!"

"That's exactly what the lecherous ol' bastard wants!" Bogie said, chuckling. "He doesn't call himself Darryl *F.* Zanuck for nothing."

I blew my top, maybe because Bogie wasn't leaping to the defense of the fair maiden who was wilting in the hot breath of the dragon of Twentieth Century-Fox. "Well, who the hell does that old bastard think he is?" I said. "I just met him this morning, and he's all over me like lint. I wouldn't go for that son of a bitch if you put a bag over his head!"

I must have been venting my anger on Bogie's toupee, flailing at it, because he said, "For God's sake, don't take it out on my damn muff; you'll wear it out! Don't get your balls in an uproar. He didn't mean anything by it. You ought to be flattered, considering those good-lookers he brought along with him for the ride."

"Yeah? Well, just because he's picking up the tab for my expenses doesn't mean he's got a *claim* on me."

Sir Bogart was not going to mount a white steed and gallop to my aid. I should have known better than to think he'd be sympathetic. I put the final touches to his toupee, and he put on his suit coat and sat down on the edge of the bed, sipping his drink and eyeing me. The smile faded from his face, and he turned very serious—or pretended to. It was needle time.

"I don't know, Pete," he said. "Maybe you've got the

wrong slant here. Maybe you should reconsider your course of action. We're talking about a movie mogul here. Play your cards right and you could be queen of Twentieth Century-Fox. Diamonds. Furs. Champagne and caviar for breakfast. Hell, it's a quick way to the top of the heap. The quickest. Most girls wouldn't turn him down, you know. I'm serious."

The phone rang.

"You're also a horse's ass," I said.

Bogie got up to answer the phone. "This is the thanks I get for trying to steer you right," he said, picking up the phone. I thought it might be Zanuck again, but it was the desk, informing us that our limousine was waiting. Zanuck was also waiting for us in front of the hotel. All three of us got into the first limousine, and it sped off toward the Denver countryside.

Zanuck looked at Bogie. "Well, you look fit and handsome in black tie," he said.

"Why shouldn't I?" Bogie said. "I *am* a handsome son of a bitch."

Then Zanuck aimed his charm at me, telling me how beautiful my gown was and how I looked like a doll.

"Thanks," I snapped. Anyone else might have been discouraged or irritated by my icy tone, but not Darryl F. Zanuck.

"You look just like a doll," he repeated.

"You've sort of got eyes for this kid of mine, haven't you, Mr. Z?" Bogie said.

"How did you guess?" Zanuck said, smiling.

Bogie looked at him a moment, studying him. "I don't think a bag would be much of an improvement, either."

Fortunately for Bogie, I was carrying a small clutch

purse. If I'd had my big handbag, I'd have slugged him with it.

"I beg your pardon?" Zanuck said.

"Never mind," I said.

But Bogie plunged on, enjoying himself. "Pete says she wouldn't go with you even if you put a bag over your head."

Zanuck laughed like hell. He was incorrigible, but I have to admit that he had a great sense of humor. "I didn't think of trying *that,*" he said.

"Well, you better watch what you do try," Bogie said. "Watch her in the clinches; she's a damn good club fighter."

"I'll keep that in mind," Zanuck said.

I said nothing.

After about a thirty-five-minute ride, the car finally pulled to a stop before an enormous colonial-style mansion. The place was crawling with servants. Inside, we were greeted by our hostess, a socialite and widow named Millie. She was a tiny woman who weighed no more than ninety pounds; she had lovely gray hair and was dressed in a magnificent evening gown. Millie was genuine. I took an immediate liking to her, and so did Bogie. She beamed with excitement at the sight of Bogie, and as they shook hands, she said, "You're my favorite actor, and I've always wanted to meet you."

Bogie played it very continental and charming. He kissed her hand, which so pleased and surprised her that she giggled aloud. One would have thought he had goosed her. Millie escorted our party through the mansion and out to the spacious garden, where at least fifty guests were seated at tables clustered around a long table at which General Eisenhower sat. We were seated with the general, but we didn't see much of him; he was always being greeted by someone or whisked away to meet someone else. He did take time during the festivities to tell Bogie that he appreciated his coming to Denver to see him.

"The pleasure's mine," Bogie said. "And if this campaign comes out a winner—and I'm sure it will—I'll meet you halfway on the greens for a game of golf."

"That's a definite date," Ike said, smiling.

Champagne and hors d'oeuvres were served, and an orchestra played. Dinner was followed by a fairly long cocktail party, during which the hostess got a little smashed. Bogie and I joined her at her table; she was seated with a fairly well-known regional novelist and screenwriter—a bachelor—and Bogie began needling him good-naturedly. I don't know whether he was needling him about one of his novels or a screenplay, but Bogie told him that he thought the love angle in the story was hollow. "You have to write from experience," Bogie said. "Hell, if you can't find love, then go to New York, where love stories are as common as the Mafia during an election campaign."

The remark was made out of Ike's earshot, but it raised quite a few eyebrows at nearby tables, which is probably why Bogie made it.

Our hostess was pleasantly pissed by now. "You tell him, Mr. Bogart," she said. "He doesn't know a damn thing about love." Then she called a servant over. "Get Mr. Bogart another pint of the extra dry," she said. Then, turning back to Bogie, "Do you have a sweetheart anywhere with hair as long and soft as mine?"

"Yeah," Bogie said. "My Baby; my wife."

"Well, then, I'd better concentrate on snaring my bachelor writer-friend here," she said.

The writer, who was one of the few at the party who wasn't dressed formally, looked a little uneasy and began rearranging his rumpled tie.

"You can't write about love worth a damn with ink," Millie said to the writer. "But you can write with my blood and break my heart whenever you please."

"Don't talk like that, Millie," the writer said. "You know I love you."

"I read you both loud and clear," Bogie said. "C'mon, Pete, four's a crowd. Let's mingle."

We strolled around and talked to people. Zanuck was out of circulation; he was in a corner talking to a broad who had the air of Cleopatra asking for Rome—gift-wrapped and delivered to her door. Zanuck was probably promising to deliver it.

General Eisenhower finally stood and asked for his coat, signaling the end of the party and time to leave for the convention hall, where he would give his address. Millie made it to the door in time to begin bidding farewell to her guests. She told Bogie that she was grateful he had come and that it would be a time she'd long remember. General Eisenhower left in the first car; we left in the second. As our car pulled away, Bogie looked back at Millie and at the other guests leaving the mansion. "There's a real lonely broad, Pete," he said. "All that money, big house, big cars, all those servants, and what good are they?"

We had box seats at the convention hall for Ike's speech. It was very exciting: an enormous hall filled to capacity; everything red, white, and blue bunting; colorful clouds of confetti; a band playing stirring music. And Ike's speech was wonderful. He wasn't a good speaker, but he was sincere and brought the crowd to its feet. The applause was thundering, and the Republican party had never been so spirited or so sure of winning as with the general.

Afterward, Zanuck threw a late supper party in the hotel ballroom for all those who had accompanied him to Denver. He was already in the ballroom, seeing to it that everything was exactly as he had ordered it, when we returned from the convention hall. He had made the seating arrangements, too. I was to sit next to him; Bogie was supposed to be seated several chairs away and across the table.

"You're all screwed up here, Mr. Z," Bogie said. "Pete's my date, you know, so you'd better seat her next to me."

Zanuck seemed nonplussed for a moment, then began altering the arrangement, moving people around. I was finally seated next to Bogie, but Zanuck had taken the chair to the other side of me. The booze flowed by the bucketful. There was great food, too, but hardly anyone ate. I dragged Bogie out on the dance floor a few times, but he was content just to sit and drink and needle people at the table—especially Zanuck. I danced with Zanuck, too. He spent the first dance trying to convince me that I should be his "girl," as he put it, rather than Bogie's. "I've got far more money than Bogart will ever have," he said.

"Listen," I said, "I've got a couple of bucks myself, so don't expect me to drool on your shoulder at the mention of money."

Zanuck thought that was hilarious. The next time on

the dance floor, he held me close and told me he'd like to give me a screen test and make me an actress.

"I've already had a screen test and I've already been an actress," I said.

"Really? What pictures did you make?"

"Actually, only one. At Republic. You remind me of the star, though. You look a lot like him from behind."

"Oh?" Zanuck said. "Who was that?"

"Hell, I don't remember," I said. "Paint or Thunderbolt or something. Who remembers horses' names?"

Zanuck cracked up. "Hell," he said, "dancing with you is like dancing with another Bogart—in skirts!"

We were still laughing when we returned to the table. Zanuck punched Bogie lightly on the arm and said, "That's quite an assistant you've got there."

"Oh, yeah?" Bogie said, turning to me. "What kind of line is the mogul giving you this time, Pete?"

"Wants to make me a star," I said, "but I think he just wants to make me, and failing that, I'd end up on the cutting-room floor."

"I think she's on to me," Zanuck said.

"That she is," Bogie said. "She's too dumb to be fooled. If you keep messing with her, she'll put a knot on your head and make you six inches taller."

"That's what she keeps telling me."

It was almost dawn before the party broke up. As usual, Bogie and I were among the last to leave. I started toward the elevator ahead of Bogie, who had paused to say good night and good-bye to several Denver people. I was waiting for Bogie in the lobby when Zanuck caught up with me. He was feeling no pain and insisted that we go up to his suite. He wouldn't take a polite no for an answer, and though he was pretty smashed, I was losing my patience with him. He was persistent as hell and grabbed me by the arm, trying to steer me into the elevator and to his suite. In his drunken state, it was inconceivable to him that a woman—any woman—would not find him irresistible. I wrenched from his grip and was just about to get the hell out of there rather than make a scene when Bogie came around the corner and saw what was happening.

Bogie had a suspicious nature, but not a jealous one; at least, that night was the only time I ever saw him exhibit jealousy. Bogie grabbed Zanuck by the arm, and for a moment, I thought he was going to slug him, but instead he pushed his face practically into Zanuck's and chewed him up one side and down the other. Among other things, he told Zanuck that if he ever laid another "claw" on me, they'd both make the morning newspapers—Bogie in the headlines and Zanuck in the obituaries.

To Zanuck, I was just another broad, so he was truly astonished at Bogie's reaction. We went up on the elevator together, Zanuck mumbling aloud about how Bogie was making a "federal case" out of a guy trying to get a little "companionship," and Bogie telling him that for fifty bucks the "cheap bastard" could arrange with the desk clerk for a little companionship. Zanuck was still mumbling—though not angry—when we got off the elevator and he went on up to his suite. We went to Bogie's suite and I took the muff off him, cleaned it, and put it back on the block before getting a couple of hours' sleep; we were scheduled for an early flight back to Los Angeles.

The next morning Zanuck looked at me suspiciously and said, "I called you after that little incident with

Bogie. Thought you'd like to have some coffee in my suite after all that booze, but you didn't answer your phone."

"I'm a sound sleeper," I said. "I didn't hear the phone ring once." I said it in truth. I didn't tell him that my phone couldn't be heard in Bogie's suite.

"Well, I'll call you when we get back to town," he said. "There are too many Bogies here."

I couldn't believe Zanuck's persistence, but I guess that's what made him the dynamo he was. Sure enough, I'd only been back in town a couple of days when I got a call from Zanuck's secretary. Mr. Z, she said, wanted me to come to his studio office around five o'clock for a conference. I knew that his secretary was used to dealing with agents, so I gave her a message with a double meaning. "Tell Mr. Zanuck that I'm sorry, but the property he's interested in isn't for sale," I said.

That's the last I heard from Darryl F. Zanuck.

I have long since become acquainted with the late Mr. Z's son, Richard, though. Richard frequents my restaurant. Like his father, he's a producer and very adept at movie making, but as a family man, he far outshines his famous father—he's a good one.

Bogie in sailor suit when he was in the Navy. (1919.
Courtesy of the Bettmann Archive.)

Clowning with George "Slim" Summerville on location for the film *Puddin' Head.* (1941)

A portrait of me taken when I was under contract at Republic Studios. (ca. 1939)

Helping Annie Sheridan in her Warner Brothers dressing room; this snapshot was taken at about the time Annie introduced me to Bogie. (ca. 1942)

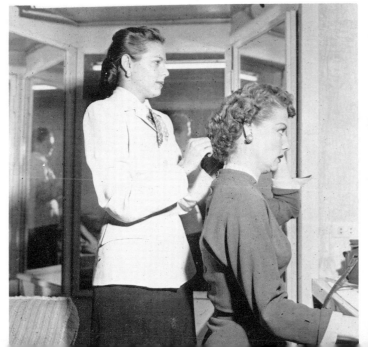

With all my Love Misty

A portrait of me taken at about the time I met Bogie. (ca. 1942)

A snapshot of me taken by Bogie. (ca. 1943)

Joe Conners, Bogie's stand-in and double, who's still an old friend. (ca. 1952)

Annie Locker and me at the salt mines in Germany. Annie was my confidante during my affair with Bogie. The crazy outfits we're wearing were required for going down into the mines. (ca. 1949)

With Ray Milland on location for a Western. (ca. 1950)

Zero Mostel entertains Bogie and me on the set of *The Enforcer* at Warner Brothers. (1951)

The studio publicity photo that I used to "autograph" with Bogie's name.
(ca. 1952)

Ethyl Barrymore, Stevie, Bacall, and me on the set of *Deadline—U.S.A.* at 20th Century-Fox. (1952)

Captain Edwin Kalbfleish, Jr. and Captain Ralph C. Anderson chat with Bogie between takes of *Battle Circus*, being filmed at Camp Pickett, Virginia. (ca. 1953)

On location at Camp Pickett, Bogie shows director Richard Brooks the award given to him by two U.S. Treasury officials for his cooperation in the War Bond Drive. (ca. 1953)

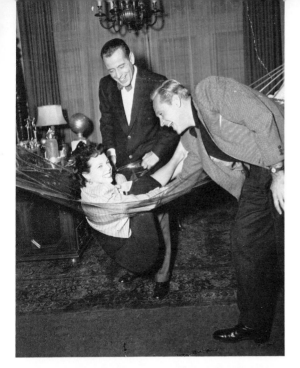

On the set of *Sabrina*, where Bill Holden and Bogie dumped me into a hammock that, for reasons I don't recall, had a hole in it. (1953)

Supervising makeup artist Hank Vallardo as he gives Bogie a trim on the set of *Sabrina* at Paramount. (1953)

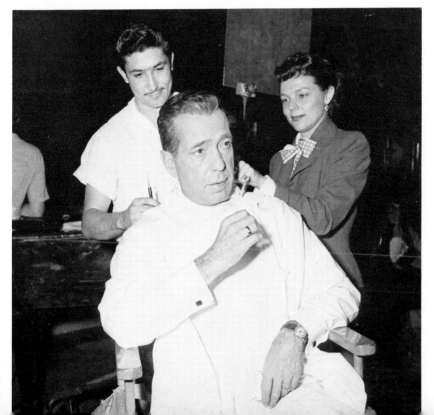

Snapshot taken by Bogie
of me aboard the *Santana*
in her slip at the San
Pedro marina. (ca. 1953)

Ava Gardner, Bogie, and
me in Rome during the
shooting of *The Barefoot
Contessa;* talk about being
eclipsed by a beautiful
woman! Bogie would have
called this a very good
photograph of me. (1954)

Giving Stevie a haircut in Bogie's dressing room; Bogie and Bacall can be seen in mirror reflection. (ca. 1954)

A snapshot of Bogie (without toupee), General Alfred M. Gruenther, and Bacall taken in Paris shortly after the filming of *The Barefoot Contessa* in Rome. (1954)

Bogie tattoos me on the set of *We're No Angels.* I have no excuse for the hat I'm wearing. (1955)

The *Santana* under sail at Cherry Cove, Santa Catalina Island. (1955)

Bogie aboard the *Santana.* (1955)

Walter and me leaving for our round-the-world honeymoon trip. (1955)

With Walter, Bob and Dixie Dunbar, and the choreographer for the Rockettes celebrating the opening of Walter's film, *So This Is Cinerama.* (1954)

Peter Ustinov, his wife, Suzanne, Walter, and me on the set of *Romanoff and Juliet*, which Walter coproduced with Peter. (1960)

A recent photo of me wishing my oldest and dearest friend, Harold Robbins, happy birthday at a party given for him by his wife, Grace, in their Beverly Hills home. (1980)

9

Public Relations

We hadn't been back from Denver long when Bogie's agent, Sam Jaffe, called to say that he had drawn up a contract with United Artists for Bogie to do a publicity tour promoting *The African Queen,* for which he had won the Oscar as Best Actor. Bogie wasn't called upon to do many such tours, but this was an Oscar-winning picture at a time when television was changing the complexion of the movie industry and cutting into box-office receipts, so United Artists, who distributed the film, wanted to protect its investment by attempting to lure television audiences back to the theaters.

Betty Bacall was busy on a film of her own and didn't make the tour with Bogie. I went along and again doubled as Bogie's hairstylist and secretary, making ticket arrangements, coordinating the itinerary, contacting friends for lunch and dinner appointments in cities we passed through, making sure that Bogie's hotel suites were stocked with an ample supply of Scotch and soda, and scheduling press interviews.

I particularly enjoyed Bogie's bouts with the press.

He was much sought after by reporters and columnists because he was always good for a remarkable quote. Bogie parried the thrusts of probing journalists as well as anyone in the business. His technique was simple and sincere: he didn't take Hollywood stardom seriously, and so his answers to questions were usually funny or satirical. News people liked his offbeat manner because they were as bored with having to ask such questions for their readers as Bogie was with having to answer them.

One of the questions inevitably asked of him whenever I was along was who I was. At first, I used to dread the question, because sometimes Bogie would reply, "That's Pete, my executive secretary and mistress." I nearly had a heart attack the first time he did this, and afterward I took issue with him about it. "Listen," he said, "don't get your balls in an uproar. Whenever a guy travels around with a good-looking secretary, people assume that they're sleeping together. Now if they *are* sleeping together, that's the last thing in the world the guy's going to admit, right? So when I tell 'em you're my mistress, a lot of them will take it for a rib. Others will think whatever they want to think, anyway, but I've added an element of doubt that didn't exist before. I mean, who the hell would be stupid enough to admit such a thing or even to raise the question if it were true?"

He was right. Most interviewers either took his answer as a joke and went on to more important and less personal questions, or they were so startled by it that they hurriedly changed the subject. In any case, it was an answer that wouldn't be printed or even pursued by the press in the fifties. Even so, I was never comfortable with the question or his answer, and I used to wince whenever it was asked.

I guess Bogie took interviews seriously early in his career, but unlike some in Hollywood who never tire of talking about themselves, he grew bored of retelling his life story and began making up stories to amuse himself. One of the questions that was most often asked of him was how he got the scar on his upper lip. It was a bad scar, and though makeup hid it quite well, it's visible if one looks for it in the close-ups in his films. There's probably enough copy written about that damn scar to fill a book or two, but as far as I know, Bogie never did give anyone a straight answer about its origin.

The story most widely circulated is that the scar marked an injury he received from shrapnel during World War One. There's no truth to the tale; Bogie joined the navy in June 1918, but he wasn't even assigned to a ship until weeks after the war ended. The version that I believe to be true, because Bogie or one of our mutual friends told me it was, is that while he was assigned to guard duty, he was given the task of escorting a prisoner from one place to another. The prisoner had his hands cuffed in front of him and, while attempting to escape, hit Bogie across the face with the handcuffs, splitting his lip.

I doubt that Bogie started the "old war wound" story; it's typical of the sort of thing Hollywood press agents used to invent—and still do—to get their clients' names in the papers. It's the kind of story Bogie would go along with, though, just for the hell of it. But the scar story I liked best was the one Bogie gave to a particularly obnoxious journalist during the *African Queen* tour.

Bogie and Me

The reporter gave us both the impression that if her city editor had had an ounce of sense, he'd have assigned a news person of her caliber to interviews with the President and heads of state rather than with movie stars like Humphrey Bogart. Bogie tolerated the insufferable woman longer than I expected, and I was astonished. He was treating her as though she were as important as she thought she was. But toward the end of the interview, she asked him about his scar. Bogie gave her first a blank expression, then a look of puzzlement. Finally he said, "What scar?"

"The one on your right upper lip," she said, staring at it while she was talking.

"Are you implying that I have a *deformity?*"

"No, of course not," she said, momentarily taken aback. "It's just that I've heard so many different accounts that—"

"Pete," Bogie interrupted, "do I have a scar on my upper lip?"

"What upper lip?" I said.

Bogie turned back to the woman journalist. "Yeah," he said, "what upper lip? Are you implying that I have an upper lip?"

In a snit, the journalist slapped her notebook closed. She was too important to be toyed with.

"Now don't get sore, ol' girl," Bogie said. "I was only joking. No sense of humor, huh? Okay, tell you what I'll do. I've been asked that same question a hundred times, and I'd like to get it laid to rest once and for all; you're just the one to do it. Actually, it's an interesting story, but a long one. I'll cut it short, though, and give you an exclusive on the real story if you promise not to misquote me."

She assured him that she'd take the story down word for word. She reopened her notebook and sat, pencil poised, as Bogie paused dramatically, apparently gathering his thoughts. "All right," he said finally, "here's the scoop. What really happened is this: a big buck-toothed broad bit me."

The woman had begun writing the first word or two, then stopped. There was a moment of silence; Bogie looked down at her notebook as though he couldn't understand why she had stopped taking notes. She looked up at him with an icy stare that could have frozen the entire room.

"The broad looked a lot like you," Bogie added, breaking the silence, and with a sincere expression. "Big, buck-toothed broad."

The woman slapped her notebook closed again and got to her feet. I guess she was so incensed that words failed her. She raised her head in indignation, and Bogie sat quietly, eyeing her coolly. "Bit me right on the lip," he added. The woman stormed from the room, and Bogie collapsed with laughter.

It was this kind of lighthearted foolishness that caused me to look forward to the promotion tour for *The African Queen.* For me, such tours were a welcome break from the often-dull business of filmmaking. Bogie wasn't exactly thrilled with the prospect of beating a publicity drum around the country (he would much rather have spent the time on his boat), but he knew that it was for his own and the industry's benefit, and it was relatively painless: parties, traveling first-class, seeing some of his old friends in New York and other cities. Then, too, it was a welcome change from early-morning calls, parts to learn, last-minute changes in script to memorize on short notice, sitting around the sound stage sometimes having to wait two or three hours to get just two or three minutes on film.

Bogie called me to put me on notice for the tour. Sam Jaffe had told him that it would include New York, Chicago, Houston, Salt Lake City, and Las Vegas. Bogie dug his heels in at the mention of Houston. "I never did like Texas," he told Sam. "Do we have to go there?"

"Yes," Sam said. "You've got a lot of fans in Texas."

Bogie continued grumbling about Texas. I never did learn what he disliked about the state—perhaps it was because the Texans he had met bragged about how their state had the biggest and best of everything, and Bogie didn't like braggarts. Ironically, Texas was one of the high points of our tour, and the Texans won Bogie's admiration.

We had been put on notice by the Jaffe office to be ready to leave at a moment's notice. United Artists didn't get their act together very quickly, though; I had been packed and ready for two days when the call finally came. A limousine would pick me up in one hour. It stopped to pick up Bogie first, then came to my Burbank place to get me, then off to Los Angeles International Airport, where we were put on a plane bound for New York.

As usual, Bogie had one drink, then slept all the way to New York. We were mobbed by news people and autograph seekers upon our arrival; we signed our way through them. I say *we* because I had to sign autographs, too. When I first started traveling with Bogie, I tried to keep from signing them. I told people that I wasn't anyone whose autograph they'd want, let alone esteem, but they simply wouldn't take my word for it.

Autograph seekers are a peculiar lot; they won't be denied, and to try is to incur their wrath. Many of them got verbally abusive when I'd refuse them. Bogie would be halfway through a cluster of autograph seekers while I'd be trailing in his wake, arguing with them, insisting that I was only his secretary, trying to dissuade them, and Bogie would say, "For Christ's sake, Pete. Sign their damn books or we'll never get out of here!" So I fell into the routine, usually using a pseudonym but occasionally signing my own name. There must be hundreds of autograph collectors who are still puzzled when they come across my name in their books.

We were finally saved from the reporters and autograph collectors by an East Coast United Artists publicity representative named Ranson. He had a limousine waiting, and we signed autographs until our bags were loaded in the limousine; then Bogie and I jumped into the back, and the limousine sped away from the crowd.

Ranson was tall and dark complexioned, with black hair. He wore a hat and a topcoat with a velvet collar. I think he was basically a nice man, but our tour was one of his first assignments for the studio, and he was pushy as hell—at first. He sat in front with the driver, and we had just pulled away from the curb when he turned in his seat and began rattling off our entire itinerary; he was to accompany us on the tour. Bogie let him ramble on for a minute or so about publicity appointments, press interviews, an appearance on the Ed Sullivan show and the like, before he finally interrupted him.

"Wait a minute, ol' boy," Bogie said. "This is Pete, my executive secretary. Now you can sit there and blab until your mouth runs dry, but I ain't paying a bit of attention to you. You get together with Pete and map all this stuff out; I'll do whatever she agrees to, but I'm not taking orders from you or anybody else, is that clear? And another thing, wise guy. It's a little soon to be thinking about all this, let alone gassing about it. What the hell do I look like, a machine? We're not even settled into our seats here, let alone our hotel, and we haven't had lunch. So just don't get your balls in an uproar. Pete and I are lunching at 21—that's the first order of business. You can call her this afternoon and get all this other crap lined out. Meanwhile, relax. You're making me nervous, and I'm not very cooperative when I'm nervous."

Ranson backed off immediately, and he did quite a good job on the rest of the trip. Bogie didn't have much regard for most public-relations people, in whom he thought hysteria was the predominant emotion; he was naturally inclined not to be manipulated by them. "Most of them are creeps," he told me, "no better than the brass they work for. All they seem to care about is their schedules, their contacts, and making themselves look good. Let them get the upper hand and they'll treat you like beef on the hoof and run you just as hard."

We unpacked and got settled in our hotel suites before leaving for lunch. Twenty-one was Bogie's favorite restaurant and his New York City headquarters, the East Coast counterpart of Romanoff's and his home away from home. He loved both places and took two- or three-hour lunches at them whenever possible.

When we left the hotel, the doorman started to whistle for a taxi, but Bogie waved him off. "Let's walk," he said. "New York is a place for walking; not like Hollywood, where you can walk your ass off and get nowhere —that's because Hollywood *is* nowhere."

Public Relations

We walked down Fifth Avenue toward 21. The streets of New York must have brought back memories for Bogie; he had never talked much of his early life there, but as we walked, he spoke of little else. He pointed out places that were important to him when he was a boy and then an aspiring young Broadway actor. "This damn place really gets to me," he said. "Makes me feel alive again."

Bogie had been born in New York City and attended Trinity School, a posh, private Presbyterian institution, before being enrolled at Phillips Academy in Andover, Massachusetts. Andover was an exclusive and expensive prep school that his father hoped would prepare him for Yale and a medical career. It wasn't to be, though. Bogie had little interest in studying and a lot of interest in extracurricular activities, like drinking, for which he was expelled after eight months. "I was a dumb son of a bitch," Bogie told me, "and if I hadn't got kicked out for drinking, I would have flunked out anyway. I left Andover under duress."

As we walked, Bogie pointed to an enormous building down a side street. "I lived in a big brownstone something like that one," he said. "It was on One Hundred and Third Street. We had a houseful, with my mother and father and me and my two kid sisters, Pat (whose real name was Frances) and Kay—and servants, too. Those were good times. We got along well as a family. About the only trouble I had with my dad was when I got kicked out of Andover; he was pretty disgusted about that. So was my mother, but we never got along too well, anyway."

Bogie's mother had been an accomplished and successful commercial artist, and one of the best known of

91

her day. She illustrated children's books and calendars and women's magazines, and prints of her works, signed with her maiden name, Maud Humphrey, are much prized by collectors today. Her most widely known sketch was one of infant Humphrey DeForest Bogart that became the logo for a brand of processed baby food (I believe Bogie told me that it was Clabber's, but I'm not sure). Bogie said that his chubby façade on all those jars of baby food became a matter of concern to his fellow students at Trinity, which resulted in his having a good many childhood fistfights in the schoolyard.

Maud Humphrey, his mother, was a matriarchal figure. Bogie said that he admired her talent and respected her, but that he couldn't say she was lovable, and what passed for artistic eccentricity was really, according to Bogie, a streak of mental instability.

"I had a pretty good childhood, though," Bogie said. "I fell in love with several of the girls next door, and as the only boy in the family, I had a lot more latitude than my sisters did. Kind of a silver-spoon life. If my dad hadn't lost his money through bad investments, I don't know what would have become of me. I had to give up my playboy days and strike out on my own, which I didn't like at all—I've always been an indolent bastard."

Bogie pointed out theaters as we walked—or places where theaters had been—in which he had performed in numerous juvenile roles on Broadway. After a year in the navy, he'd gotten a job with William A. Brady, a neighbor of the Bogarts who owned The Playhouse, a legitimate theater on Forty-eighth Street. In time, Brady, who was also a producer, made Bogie the road manager for a play called *The Ruined Woman.* Bogie, caustic even then, passed his time backstage needling the actors and actresses for having to do so little to earn their keep. It seemed to him that acting was so easy that getting paid for it was tantamount to stealing. But he soon discovered that things aren't always what they seem. One of the supporting actors couldn't go on one night, and Bogie, who had heard the play from the wings so often that he knew all the parts by heart, was pressed into service by the actors he had been needling.

"I had only one line, as I recall," Bogie said, "so when I heard my cue, I strode onstage full of youthful and stupid confidence, took one look at the audience, delivered my line, and peed my pants—right there onstage. I was so scared that I simply lost control of my bladder. In that one humiliatingly wet moment, I realized why those people were making two or three times the amount I was, and why they deserved to be making even more. Acting's a tough and honorable profession, and anyone who says it isn't either hasn't done it or isn't doing it right."

Bogie was in dozens of plays before he got his first big break. Stuart Rose, a beau of his sister Pat (Stuart and Pat later married, and Stuart became editor of *The Saturday Evening Post*) was the New York story editor for William Fox Studios, and he arranged for Bogie to have a screen test. That was in 1930. The Fox executives liked what they saw, and Bogie was summoned to Hollywood, where he was given a few bit parts and was largely ignored until his contract ran out. Bogie returned to New York a failure—in his own eyes, anyway. His lack of success was magnified by the stage successes of actress Mary Philips, his second wife and the one to whom he was married at the time. For several months after the Hollywood reversal, Bogie did little but drink.

He finally did return to the stage, and, after appearing in many unsuccessful plays, he won critical acclaim portraying Duke Mantee in Robert Sherwood's play *The Petrified Forest,* starring Leslie Howard. The play opened in January 1935; Bogie got smash reviews for his chilling performance, but when Warner Brothers bought the film rights, they planned to star Howard and to give Bogie's part to Edward G. Robinson. Leslie Howard, who had returned to his native England for a brief vacation, wired Warner Brothers, refusing to do the picture unless Bogie, whose work he respected, was cast as Mantee. Bogie was given another Warner Brothers contract, and the film launched his movie career; he never returned to the stage.

Bogie and Leslie Howard remained the closest of friends, and more than fifteen years later, Bogie named his second child, a daughter, Leslie Howard Bogart, after the actor. One of Bogie's biggest disappointments was that his father, Dr. Belmont DeForest Bogart, died in 1935, just a few weeks before *The Petrified Forest* opened; Bogie worshipped his father, who would have taken great pride in his son's success.

I had made lunch reservations at 21 in Bogie's name, and when we arrived, Chuck, the doorman, greeted us warmly. Inside, the entire 21 staff swarmed around us. We were shown to Bogie's favorite table and served loudmouth on the house. Waiters came over to shake Bogie's hand; others gravitated to the table, too, including an associate of Louella Parsons. She eyed me and asked pointedly where Betty was. "Busy on a picture," Bogie told her.

"And who is this?" the associate asked in a tone that really said: *what* is this?

Bogie caught the tone, too, and I braced for his answer. "Wouldn't you like to know," he said.

The woman raised an eyebrow. "A mystery woman?"

"Yeah," Bogie said. "Just say she's my mystery woman mistress."

"My goodness. Do you really want me to print that?"

"Anything you like," Bogie said.

I thought the woman might be an exception to Bogie's theory about news people; I had visions of headlines in 120-point bold hysterics, but instead it was a small item in the following day's paper:

> Who was the attractive mystery
> woman that Bogart was lunching
> with at 21? What's happened to
> his Baby?

Baby, of course, was Bogie's pet name for Betty Bacall.

Nunnally Johnson, the great writer-director, was having lunch at 21, too. The Johnsons and the Bogarts were very close, and their children went to school together. Nunnally was always kidding Bogie about his drinking and about the alcohol in his "thermostat." "So how's the alcohol registering?" he asked.

"Barely visible," Bogie said, "but I should tie one on, blow the thermostat through the top, and watch our PR man go to pieces. I won't, though."

Nunnally discussed Bogie's tour, then was off to an appointment. Bogie and I ordered oysters for lunch (he didn't always order ham and eggs), then walked back to the hotel, where he took his usual after-lunch nap while I got on the phone to Ranson and worked out the tour schedule with him—much to his relief. I think he feared that Bogie would be totally uncooperative. He didn't know that Bogie was the consummate professional.

Bogie was scheduled to appear that night on "The Ed Sullivan Show," the most popular television variety show of its day, so Ranson went over to the network that afternoon to make arrangements while I set up a cocktail party that Bogie wanted to host for a few of his friends who were in town, including agent Irving "Swifty" Lazar and film producer Sam Spiegel and Walter Thompson (whom I would marry a few years later). Walter was an international film executive with Cinerama Corporation and an independent director and producer (*Romanoff and Juliet,* with Peter Ustinov, was among the many films he produced). Walter kept an apartment in New York City but spent most of his time in Europe, Asia, and South America. I had been having an affair with Walter for a couple of years, and I introduced him to Bogie; they often discussed forming a motion picture production company together, but Bogie died before anything came of it.

The cocktail party lasted a couple of hours. Naturally, it was all picture-business talk. Someone mentioned Western films, and Bogie recalled doing a Western in 1939 with James Cagney called *The Oklahoma Kid.* Bogie said that neither he nor Cagney should have played Westerns. "Wearing that damn huge Western hat," Bogie said, "Cagney looked like a mushroom."

As always, Swifty Lazar was in top form, joking, telling show-business stories, kidding around with Bogie. Bogie liked Swifty very much. "He's a tough li'l character," Bogie used to say of him. "Little, but mighty." As an agent, Swifty has put together incredible deals that have made his clients (and him) rich and that his competitors have looked upon with a mixture of awe and jealousy. Although Bogie and Swifty were good friends, Swifty never represented Bogie. It's a tribute to Bogie's loyalty that he stayed with his agent, Sam Jaffe, and a tribute to Swifty that he never tried to take business advantage of his friendship with Bogie.

Bogie used to kid me about Swifty, saying that the two of us should get together because we were about the same size (about 5′3″) and would make a good pair of bookends or something. "There's no chance, though," Bogie would say. "Swifty likes those tall showgirls; you ain't his type. You're too short and dirty for him." And with Bogie's penchant for ribbing, he eventually turned his own words around and attributed them to me. "Pete says you're too short and dirty for her," he once told Swifty. I often see Swifty these days, but I've never asked him about the incident. I doubt that he really believed that I had said that about him; he was wise to Bogie's ribs and probably discounted the whole thing.

While I was talking to Swifty, Sam Spiegel tried to talk Bogie into playing a priest in one of his upcoming productions. Bogie laughed at the idea at first but finally said he might consider it. Spiegel later asked Walter to keep after Bogie to play the part. Bogie liked Spiegel, too, and that made him one of Bogie's targets.

A couple of years later, when Bogie was in Italy filming *Beat the Devil,* a journalist asked what kind of part he was playing in the picture. "I play an adventurer," Bogie said, "a charlatan, kind of a dressed-up Sam Spiegel."

When we arrived at the television studio to do the Ed Sullivan show, Bogie and I met Ed backstage. It was my first meeting with Sullivan, and I was surprised at his wit and humor; I had expected him to be much as he appeared onstage, rather stiff and a little dour. I believe it was Bogie's first meeting with Sullivan, too, but they hit it off immediately and began kidding each other. "People tell me we look alike," Bogie said to him. "It must be because we both have swell hair. We're neither young nor handsome, yet we're still much sought after as leading men; maybe that's why they compare us."

"I don't know that we're alike," Sullivan said. "I hear you're a whiskey drinker who seems warmed and comforted by disturbing the peace in the wee hours of the morning. And what about that incident of a few years ago at El Morocco, where you're supposed to have knocked down a shapely young woman?"

"Oh, that," Bogie said. "Well, I was a little drunk, but she was trying to steal my kid's panda and I was trying to extricate myself and the panda from her—you would've done the same thing under those circumstances. Like the referee says, 'Protect your panda at all times.' Besides, as I said, I was a little drunk; everyone's drunk at four in the morning, or should be if they're stupid enough to stay up that late."

"I'm not at all sure we're alike in that respect, Mr. Bogart," Sullivan said.

"That's only because nobody's tried to steal your

panda," Bogie said. "And don't give me that Irish ma-
larkey. I've got a habit of fracturing Hollywood taboos
with regularity, but it seems to me that you do a pretty
good job of that yourself here on the East Coast."

They both laughed and continued ribbing each other
until showtime. Walter and I sat out front and watched
the show, and after Bogie appeared to plug *The African
Queen,* the three of us went to 21 for drinks, then on
to La Veloise for dinner, then to Walter's apartment,
where we sat on the balcony overlooking the Hudson
and had brandy before Bogie left to get a good night's
sleep. I didn't get back to the hotel until about four, but
I was up by seven and calling Ranson to check on our
flight to Chicago, which was our next stop. Ranson said
we were to leave later that afternoon.

Bogie called at eight. "Get over here, ol' girl," he
said. "It's Bloody Mary time."

I went to his suite, mixed us Bloody Marys, and ordered breakfast from room service. Then we packed for
Chicago, and I put Bogie's cocktail muff on him before
we checked out of the hotel and walked to 21, where
we were meeting Walter for lunch. It wasn't until we
met Walter and I was sitting next to him, across from
Bogie, that Bogie noticed the diamond necklace I was
wearing. "Jesus Christ!" he said. "What's that on your
neck? It's practically putting my eyes out!"

"A going-away present from Walter," I said.

"Christ, you old goat," Bogie said to Walter. "You're
really making it tough for me, buying her that stuff.
Next thing I know she'll be wanting a raise. I'm gonna
have to have a little private talk with you about this
later." Bogie had dubbed Walter "the old goat," owing
to his premature streak of gray—almost white—hair.

Walter didn't mind the sobriquet at all and began referring to himself as an old goat, too.

We said good-bye to Walter and took the limousine to the airport. Walter's present had got Bogie thinking. "You going to marry that old goat, Pete?" he said.

"I don't know."

Bogie leaned over and kissed me, then held my hand. "I had hoped we could work out something and be together," he said. "I do love you, you know."

"I know, darling," I said. "We're one of those two-ships-passing-in-the-night basket cases, I guess—a couple of lousy navigators. Maybe we'll get together in our next lives."

"Well, they can't say we haven't lived, kid—in this one, I mean."

We both fell silent for a while. I had all but given up hope now that Bogie's children, too, had come between us. Bogie now had two—Leslie and Stephen—with Betty Bacall. I took some comfort in the fact that Bogie had at least found someone he was relatively happy with. In dark moments, I thought I was stupid for finding comfort there, but, in fact, I could never be totally selfish with regard to Bogie. God knows I tried to be. It was certainly not in my best interest that he seemed happy with Betty or that their marriage would last. Talk about tangled webs!

"Walter's an okay guy," Bogie said. "You couldn't do any better than marrying him. And he couldn't do any worse."

"Thanks a lot, you smooth talker," I said. I was kidding with him about it, but I took pride in his statement. I was happy that I had at last found a guy that Bogie approved of. Not that I needed his approval, but

Bogie was an excellent judge of character, and it just made me happy that he, too, shared my liking for Walter Thompson. As to marrying Walter, I didn't know. I had almost given up hope of a life with Bogie—though I couldn't bring myself entirely to face that possibility.

Our next stop was Chicago, where Bogie did very little to win the Windy City's affection. I've always liked Chicago, but Bogie professed hatred for it and couldn't be dissuaded. As we circled the airport, Bogie looked out and said, "This is a lousy city, Pete—not the people, but the city. It's the only one in the country that's *adjusted* to crime as part of its social pattern. That's pathetic. It's no better today than in the days of Capone, Siegel, and Lizzy Allen's House of Mirrors whorehouse. These people deserve better, but they're never going to get it."

As the ramp was wheeled up for us to get off the plane, members of the Chicago press rushed it and jostled for position, waiting for Bogie. They crowded around the foot of the ramp and were so determined to keep their positions that they blocked the exit for the plane's other passengers. Ranson saved the day—and perhaps a battle, because the passengers were getting very angry with the press—by working his way down the ramp and persuading the news people that he had made arrangements for a press conference at the hotel and that Bogie would absolutely refuse to talk to them until the press conference.

A Chicago publicity representative met us with a limousine. Unfortunately, he fit Bogie's conception of Chicago: he was short, heavy-set, and rather sinister-looking, the kind that any casting director would have given a machine gun and put in a gangster picture.

Bogie elbowed me. "See what I mean?" he said. "The bastard's probably packing a rod, too."

We were taken to the Bismarck Hotel and met at the door by the hotel's owner, Mr. Otto Idle, who was of Swiss descent and a very nice man. He showed us to our suites, then invited us for a drink at the Palmer Club. "Okay," Bogie said, "but first I've got to have some Scotch and soda up here. I can't take this city cold sober."

Idle smiled and ordered his personnel to action; within minutes, Bogie had enough Scotch and soda in his suite—on the house—to throw a good-size cocktail party. We had a drink, freshened up, met Mr. Idle in the Palmer bar for hors d'oeuvres and more drinks, then went over to the Swiss Châlet room for the press conference. By this time, Bogie was feeling pretty good and had forgotten his animosity toward Chicago for the moment. The faces of the news people were different, but the questions were the same. I could understand why Bogie insisted on his supply of loudmouth. Even the prospect of *listening* to those same questions and answers over and over again was enough to drive me to drink, and I didn't have to answer them as Bogie did. Bogie played the interview pretty straight, as United Artists had contracted him to do, but he enlarged on different questions in each city to keep from getting totally bored.

"How'd you like working with Katharine Hepburn?"

"When we first started shooting, I thought Katie was nuts," Bogie said. "I couldn't stand her. But I soon changed my mind. She's an okay broad and a damned good actress. The location was rugged, the bugs and heat unbearable, and we had every conceivable technical difficulty, but she didn't complain once."

"How was the food?"

"Awful. But there was plenty of Scotch, which made me forget about the food. It was good for medicinal purposes, too. Besides, I was playing a drunken river-boat captain."

"How'd you get supplies into the jungle?"

"By private plane."

"Were there many wild animals?"

"I never saw so many animals at close range in my life: crocodiles, hippos, snakes, wild boar, elephants, and the biggest damn ants in the world; the ants drove us completely out of one camp."

"What about the English crew?"

"Oh, I wouldn't consider them animals," Bogie said. That got a laugh from the press.

"I'd work with the English bunch anytime," Bogie added. "They were a damn rugged group and tops in their craft. Many of them came down with malaria, and we had a hell of a time trying to get them to stop working even with their fits of fever."

"Those leeches that were on you in the picture, were they real?"

"They sure as hell were. Real rubber. I damn near wore them out by the time the picture was completed."

"Where in Africa was the picture shot?"

"We had a small camp on the Rufyi. Bamboo, thatch roofs, buckets with holes in them for showers. We had about eighty people down there and did most of our shooting on a huge raft made of planks and native grass; the water leaked in a little, but we just bailed it out and kept going."

"Your wife, Lauren Bacall, went with you on location. How did she like it?"

"She's a goddamned rugged and cheerful broad and never once complained."

"Was the African location as rough as the Mexican location for *The Treasure of the Sierra Madre?*"

"Hell, yes. Just as rough and just as dirty and hot. But the hardships of locations give character to the pictures, I believe. And where the going is rough, it's important that the people working on them like each other and get along. We were lucky to have a good cast and crew on both pictures."

"Didn't Huston direct both pictures?"

"Right. John Huston directed them both; in fact, he appeared in the opening scenes of *Treasure.* He played the American in the white suit that I kept bumming pesos from. Huston's a good writer and actor and the best damn director in the business. Henry Blanke was the executive producer, and he's the only real executive producer we've got in the business."

After the press conference, we went to the Tavern Club with Mr. Idle; it was an elegant place high above Michigan Avenue, with a grand view of the city. The Chicago publicity man introduced Bogie to some visiting United Nations diplomats. One of them had a drink with us and looked out at the magnificent view. "This is one of the finest cities in your country," he said to Bogie.

"You're dead wrong," Bogie said. "This is one of the lousiest cities in my country. Chicagoans ought to move out of here and let the gangsters fight it out until they knock themselves off. What they've done to this city is unspeakable and sure as hell not typically American."

Public Relations

The next morning we headed for Houston, Texas. Bogie anticipated the move with almost as much dread as he had felt at the prospect of visiting Chicago. When the plane landed and we started down the ramp, a large marching band struck up "The Eyes of Texas Are Upon You," and the Texas Rangerettes performed in their colorful red-white-and-blue jackets, white slacks, and white Stetson hats. Ranson said, "This is quite a reception for you."

Bogie looked at him in disbelief. "For me?" he said. "Did you arrange all this?"

"Nope. The Texans did."

"I'll be damned," Bogie said. "I thought the President or someone was aboard."

Houston's mayor met us at the foot of the ramp and presented Bogie and me with white Stetsons and keys to the city; I was given a key because I was with him. And after we all had our pictures taken together, we got into the mayor's car and were escorted through the city to our hotel; the band led the way. "We want to make your stay in Houston a memorable one, Mr. Bogart," the mayor said.

"Christ," Bogie said, "I'd have to be a total ingrate to forget a reception like this—even if I'm not deserving of such attention."

We were taken to Houston's most fashionable and exclusive hotel, which boasted, among other things, Chanel perfume room deodorizers. Out of deference to the hotel, I'll not name it, but upon our arrival, an influential man I'll call Tex met us there. He was in his early forties at the time, tall, broad-shouldered, and muscular. He weighed about two hundred pounds and was very handsome, with heavily lashed, wide-set eyes and a deep tan from the blazing Texas sun. It was said that he owned the hotel, half of Houston, and most of the oil beneath and around it—undoubtedly an exaggeration, but he was certainly rich. He was also a notorious ladies' man, and from his looks alone, I judged that he had no trouble attracting women.

When we arrived at the hotel, Tex strode across the enormous lobby with a slow, easy gait and grabbed Bogie's hand, pumping it vigorously and damn near mangling it. "Glad to see you again, tough guy!" he said.

Bogie looked up at him quizzically, unable to remember having met him, and Tex reminded him of where and when they had met before. "Oh, yeah," Bogie said. "Of course. How the hell could I forget a tall son of a bitch like you?"

Bogie introduced me to Tex, who looked me up and down and said, "You better keep your eye on this one, Mr. Bogart, or I'm liable to put my brand on her and keep her here in Texas."

"Don't let her size fool you," Bogie told him. "That would be like putting fire to dynamite—that comes in small packages, too, you know. She's half-Mexican and half-Irish, and when she gets mad, everybody with sense dives for cover."

"Damn!" Tex said, eyeing me even more closely than before. "That's a mighty powerful combination: Mexican and Irish."

"Powerful?" Bogie said. "It's lethal!"

We were herded immediately into a large banquet room that Tex had set up for a press conference. Bogie spent about an hour answering questions, then another half-hour or so being introduced to people by Tex. I spent my time talking to a newsman who seemed an expert on Tex and his family. "He attracts women like a magnet," the newsman said admiringly. "Women can't resist him. Of course, being a multimillionaire and owning half of Texas doesn't exactly scare women off. But getting any woman he wants has kind of spoiled him—he's got a weakness for women. He's a good ol' boy, though."

Bogie finally signaled to Ranson that he should break the party up diplomatically. He was tired from the trip from Chicago and wanted to get a little rest before joining Tex and the others for dinner, drinks, and dancing in the grand ballroom—a little party Tex had arranged in Bogie's honor. Ranson did his best to clear the room, but the press wasn't budging. Tex had furnished an open and free bar, and most of the news people weren't leaving while there was still liquor in the bottles, so Bogie, Ranson, and I slipped up to our suites to unpack and relax before the evening's festivities.

At seven thirty I put Bogie's cocktail muff on him and we joined Tex in the hotel bar, where a dozen of Tex's millionaire friends had gathered to meet Bogie. They were all straightforward and genuine, and Bogie liked them. We had a drink or two, then moved en masse to the gold ballroom, where there was an orchestra for dancing and where the main table had been set for dinner. Tex made the seating arrangements, putting me on one side of him and Bogie on the other. After dinner, the whiskey and champagne began flowing, and Tex kept having bottles of bourbon and Scotch brought over to the table. He insisted on pouring the drinks for everyone; the third and fourth were larger and stronger than the first and second, and soon no one at the table was feeling any pain.

Bogie was captivated by the woman who had been seated beside him. Her name was Eunice, and she was known around those parts as Queen of the Range. Eunice was in her early fifties and was a real ranch woman: tall and heavy-set, with a cheerful and leathery face that was probably the color and texture of her saddle. She ran a large cattle ranch and employed a small army of ranch hands; she had lost her husband a few years earlier. "He was riding the range and his damn horse stepped into a gopher hole and broke his leg," Eunice told Bogie. "Then the goddamn son of a bitch fell and rolled over on my husband and killed him."

Eunice wasn't drinking any of the stuff that Tex was serving. She had a bottle of Wild Turkey under her chair, and as the evening passed, she'd reach down and drink straight from the bottle. She offered Bogie a swig, but he begged off, saying that he drank only Scotch.

"It's got to be a tough life, running a ranch like that," Bogie said to her.

"It's a lot of hard work, all right," she said, "but not half as bad as this city life. Only reason I'm here now is to meet you, Mr. Bogart. Ain't many movie stars I'd come clear in here to see. You and Duke Wayne, maybe."

"Well, I'm glad you made the trip. And never mind the *Mister* stuff; call me Bogie."

"I see your movies whenever I can. I always like them because you don't take any bullshit from anybody."

"The credit should go to the writers," Bogie said. "I just act out what they write, you know."

"Hell, I know that! I ain't stupid, you know, Mr. Bogie. What I'm talking about is here," she said, thumping the ample breast over her heart. "And that comes through even on film, you know, like with Duke Wayne, too. But to hell with this. Let's dance."

She dragged Bogie out on the dance floor and turned him every way but loose. They danced for about half an hour, and she had Bogie laughing constantly. He really enjoyed himself, but he said later that he had a hell of a time trying to keep her from doing the leading while they danced. He had about fifty pounds of breasts hanging over his head, and she nearly danced him to death. Eunice is too old to be riding the range now—though it wouldn't surprise me to learn that she still is—but I hope she's still out there barking orders from her rocking chair on the porch.

Later, a beautiful brunet, who was a model and buyer for a Houston department store, latched onto Bogie. She gave him the eye and suggested that they leave the party so that she could show him the sights of Houston, alone. But Bogie preferred Eunice's company and told her that Eunice was his date for the evening.

While Bogie was busy with Eunice, I danced with Tex. I came about up to his belt buckle. He came on pretty strong, as he did with all women, wanting to know about my love life—the usual routine. But he was drinking straight bourbon by the tumblerful, and he was getting drunker by the moment. Finally, we sat down to rest from dancing, and he said, "Believe I'll take me a little nap." I assumed that he intended on retiring to his suite, but instead he simply slumped forward and thumped his head down on the table. He was out like a light.

It wasn't until Bogie asked me to dance and I started to get up that I realized Tex had gone to sleep with a handful of my evening gown locked in his viselike grip. "Wait a minute," I told Bogie, "I've got to extricate myself here."

Bogie and I were both looking down, amused, while I tried to pull from Tex's grip, when Eunice saw what I was doing and jumped out of her chair. "M'gawd!" she said. "Don't do that!"

We both looked up at her in surprise. "Don't even move," she said. "The first thing you gotta learn about Tex is never to wake him when he's been drinking; he comes out of it throwin' those hamhock fists of his in all directions at once like he was being bushwhacked by a bunch of Democrats. I saw him take out two waiters and one of his own boys one night before he came to his senses and realized what he was doing."

We all looked at Tex. He had slumped down in his chair and was now practically under the table, sleeping soundly, my skirts firmly locked in his big fist. Eunice called one of the waiters over. I figured she had summoned him to help me, but instead she said to him, "You tell that son of a bitch behind the bar to quit serving us cheap whiskey. Look what it's done to Tex here!"

Bogie thought my predicament was funny as hell. I would have slugged him myself if I could have gotten out of Tex's grip alive just then. It took some talking, but Bogie finally got a couple of Tex's boys to come to my aid. I was freed without incident, and we left Tex, still asleep and sinking further under the table. I stayed with Bogie that night, and it's a good thing I did. We learned from the bellhop that Tex had finally awakened and had disturbed a good many hotel guests at about four A.M., pounding on the door to my suite. When I didn't answer, he got a key, only to find the room empty.

The bellhop related the incident with pleasure. It was just another—and not an unusual—incident in the colorful life of his legendary boss, whom he obviously admired.

"Yeah, we figured that might happen," Bogie told the bellhop, "so our PR man gave my secretary his suite and slept on the couch in mine."

The bellhop eyed Bogie skeptically. "Un-huh," he said, "good thinking."

Later Bogie said, "That damn kid's too ignorant to be fooled, Pete."

We left Tex a thank-you note for his hospitality and were on our way to Salt Lake City before he probably even awoke. After all the drinking we had done the night before, we were sorely in need of a pick-me-up and looked forward to the press conference, which was to be held in the airport's VIP lounge. There was no one waiting for us when we got off the plane. "A little quiet here," Bogie said. "But then after that reception they gave us in Texas, even landing in a war zone would seem dull. Those Texans are real people."

A Mr. Cox, who seemed to be in charge of the press corps, met us in the airport and escorted us to the lounge where the press was waiting. "We have refreshments on the table over here, Mr. Bogart," he said, leading us to a table of hors d'oeuvres, soft drinks, and coffee.

"Where the hell's the booze?" Bogie said.

"Oh, we don't have any liquor, Mr. Bogart," Cox said. "Utah's a dry state."

"Good God, man!" Bogie said. "Are you serious?"

"Yessir. I thought everyone knew that."

"Ranson!" Bogie yelled.

Ranson hurried over. He had never heard Bogie raise his voice like that—neither had I—and he was alarmed.

"Did you know this is a dry state?" Bogie said.

"Huh?"

"Never mind," Bogie said. "Either get me out of here or get me a bottle of Scotch. No Scotch, no work."

While Ranson scooted about looking for a bottle, Bogie circulated among the news people. One of them asked him what he thought of Salt Lake City. "I haven't seen much of it yet," Bogie said, "except for Bryce Canyon, which we flew over, and the airport here, but if it's really as dry as I'm told it is, I'm not going to like it."

"Well, it's dry all right," the newsman said.

"Then you can quote me as saying that I find the city primitive. Any city or state that makes it unlawful for an adult to choose whether he wants to drink or not is uncivilized. People are going to drink anyway, and all the legislators are doing in this state is ensuring that otherwise law-abiding citizens will have police records."

"You won't get an argument from me there," the newsman said. "But I imagine a few bottles will turn up for you, Mr. Bogart."

Sure enough, Ranson returned with a bottle of Scotch and some soda water. And Bogie, drink in hand, opened the press conference.

When the press meeting was over, we were driven into town. Ranson was put in charge of the bottle of Scotch, and Bogie watched him and the liquor like a hawk. A representative of the city rode with us and took us on a little motor tour, pointing out the sights, including the area where Brigham Young, the founder of the city, is reported to have said, "This is the place."

"Yeah, this is the place, all right," Bogie sneered. "And it's as goddamn dry as the day Brigham Young stumbled in here."

Everything our guide told us about the city was twisted by Bogie into a criticism of the dry state, dry city, and dry people. When we were told that Young, as was the Mormon custom then, had a dozen or so wives, Bogie said, "Jesus! One wife is more than enough for any man to handle, let alone a dozen. And just think, Pete, he didn't drink, either."

After all the day's appointments were fulfilled, we went back to our hotel, and Bogie lit into Ranson for booking us into a city where drinking was against the law. "I wouldn't do that to a dog," Bogie said. I had never seen him so mad. After about half an hour of listening to him rant, I slipped out and went over to my own suite for some peace and quiet. I was just thinking about turning in and getting a good night's sleep— which I really needed after that nonstop Houston party —when the phone rang.

"C'mon over for a smash of loudmouth," Bogie said.

"Okay," I said, "but only one. I've got to get some sleep. Those Texans wore me to frazzle."

"Me, too," Bogie said, "but I was just standing here and having a drink. You know, this city doesn't look so bad under cover of darkness and under the influence of alcohol."

When I got to his suite, Ranson was gone—and was probably still trying to get the ringing out of his ears— but there were two new bottles of Scotch, ice, and soda on the table. Bogie was standing at the window, looking down at the city traffic. "Fix yourself a smash," he said. Then he turned back to the window. "We're leaving for Las Vegas first thing in the morning."

I made a drink and started to sit down. "Come here and look at all these people down here, Pete," Bogie said. "Every one of these sons-a-bitches is stone cold sober. This whole city is sober—the whole state, even. Can you imagine that? We're surrounded by sober! It's terrifying!"

He was playing it for laughs, of course, but he was noticeably relieved when our plane was airborne the next morning.

Las Vegas was a study in contrasts. We were met in the airport lobby by two leathery-faced men dressed in jeans, white short-sleeve shirts, and Stetsons, who nodded at us in a friendly fashion and told us they were the press. "We just wanted to get a couple of photographs of you, Mr. Bogart," they said.

We were driven by limousine to Wilbur Clark's Desert Inn, where we were met by Mr. Clark himself. He ordered our bags sent to our suites and invited us to have a drink with him. Bogie told Clark of our "terrible" experience at what Bogie called "the end of the earth—the dry end," and Clark joked with him about it.

"Say, ol' girl," Bogie said to me, "doesn't Mr. Clark here remind you of someone we know?"

"Yes," I said. "Walter Thompson."

To my surprise, Clark said he had known Walter for years.

It was quiet and cool and comfortable in the bar lounge, and Bogie settled in to relax after the rigors of the publicity tour. This was our last stop before returning home. We ordered another drink, and Clark excused himself and went about his rounds at the hotel and casino. Bogie gave me two silver dollars. "See if you can win us another round of drinks," he said.

I went over to the craps table and watched the gamblers play for a few minutes. I didn't know anything about the game, but I finally put the two dollars down on something—I don't even know what—and won fifty dollars. I got all excited about winning and hurried back to the bar to show Bogie. "Beginner's luck," he said. "But it's enough to keep us in drinks for a while."

Bogie eyed the gamblers from our booth in the bar, then finally took two silver dollars and said, "I'll see if I can win us another round or two." He was back shortly. "Crapped out," he said. "I better stick to acting and sailing."

A while later I tried the dollar slot machines and won eighty dollars. We had more than a hundred dollars in winnings, and finally Bogie said, "What the hell. A person only gets to Vegas once in a while. Let's see how long we can go with this money. With your luck and my looks we might break the house—at least we'll have some fun trying."

It was daybreak the following morning before we finally quit—about a hundred dollars ahead. Then we got a few hours' sleep and took the afternoon flight back to Los Angeles. It took us both several days to recover from the brief tour. "Thank God I had you with me," Bogie told me. "Otherwise I would have jumped that damned tour and gotten into hot water with United Artists."

As for me, I was sorry it was over—as usual. Promotion tours and location shootings were the only times that I had Bogie all to myself for any length of time, the only periods we ever had anything resembling married life, and I treasured such times. I always broke down at the end of each location shooting and each trip we took together. It got so that Bogie would anticipate my melancholy mood—which usually overcame me the day before he was to return to Betty—and he'd try to help me through it by being even more attentive and loving than usual. I used to get mad at myself for falling into those damn melancholy fits, but Bogie never did. He knew I couldn't help myself. I'm really not much of a whiner and crier, but I never did learn to control the tears whenever it came time to part with Bogie after having him all my own for a while.

10

At the Studio

At seven A.M., the phone rang in Bogie's bungalow dressing room at Paramount Pictures. It was Mike, the gate guard. "The tough guy just drove through," he said.

I thanked him and immediately put in a call to makeup, informing them of Bogie's arrival, then turned back to the task at hand: preparing Bogie's toupee. It was always kept mounted on a wooden block, which was hewn to the exact shape of Bogie's head. At the end of each shooting day, the lace of the toupee had to be thoroughly cleaned of adhesive in wig solvent, then placed on the block, where it was combed and pinned to hold its shape. I removed the pins each morning and gave it another combing preparatory to its application; it was a part of my morning routine that never varied.

The making of films is an early-morning business and is not at all glamorous. The cast and crews may change from one picture to another, but all else is constant: slow and often boring beyond belief—except for occasional personality conflicts among the participants and the ribs devised to ward off boredom. Otherwise, if you've seen one film being made, in a sense, you've seen them all. For this reason, I've rarely made notes concerning the films I've worked on, even though I've kept a journal of sorts since I first came to Hollywood.

I do have entries in my journals relating to the making of *Sabrina* in 1954, though, because it was noteworthy as Bogie's first Paramount picture and we were in new quarters. (Bogie later made *We're No Angels* and *The Desperate Hours* for Paramount, too; I worked on them both.) Bogie had done mostly location pictures in Africa, Italy, and Hawaii after leaving the Warner Brothers lot, except for *Sirocco*, which he did for Columbia, and *Battle Circus*, which he did for MGM. *Sabrina* is as good a film as any to give one an impression of what Bogie's workaday life was like during a studio shooting.

Bogie's Paramount quarters were called a bungalow dressing room, but they weren't in a bungalow; they were housed in a long, two-story building on the edge of the lot. The ground-floor units were large and reserved for the stars; the second-story units were less elaborate and accommodated supporting actors and actresses. Bogie's ground-floor quarters had two big dressing rooms with baths, a large living room furnished in good taste, and a small kitchenette, complete with a range and a refrigerator. The kitchenette served as our bar. We kept the refrigerator stocked with beer, for Bogie always had a bottle of beer with his lunch, and the shelves above the countertop were stocked with bottles of vodka, bourbon, and loudmouth for afternoon smashes. The range was used only for making coffee, which on this particular morning was mercifully burbling in the percolator, its aroma permeating the quarters and giving promise that, with its aid, I might make it through the day.

I had just set the coffee mugs out on the counter when Bogie came in, cheerful and smiling, as he always was in the morning. "Morning, Pete. That coffee smells good and strong. How about a cup of it?"

As usual, he sat down at the makeup table and opened his script to take a look at the scenes to be shot that day. Bogie rarely took his script home; he was what in the business is called a quick study. He had a photographic mind, I think, and could learn an entire page of dialogue with one reading. He also had an astonishing memory; if he didn't have time to go over his script before reporting to the set, he'd call for a run-through or two before they shot the scene, and in that length of time, he'd know not only his own lines but those of everyone else as well.

Films are not done in sequence like plays, of course. A director may choose to begin somewhere in the middle of the script, then skip back and forth, leaving to the film cutters and editor the job of splicing the sequences into proper order. For this reason, Bogie usually scanned the script each morning, not so much to learn his lines but to get the mood and feel of the story once again, so he'd know what he was supposed to have been through—as the character he was portraying—before he did the scenes that were to be shot that day. He had enormous powers of concentration, which he attributed to his early stage experience; he had never taken acting lessons.

I poured a cup of coffee and placed it before him on the makeup table. Absorbed with the script, he took a big swig of the coffee and screwed his face up like a prune. "Jesus!" he said, looking into the cup. "What the hell is this stuff you've brewed? Some kind of Arizona cowboy coffee?"

"I need it strong this morning, Bogie."

"Strong! It'll take over the entire studio if we don't keep an eye on it!" He looked up at me. "Do I detect a hangover lurking about?"

"Not lurking," I said. "It's a full-fledged assault. I didn't even have time to sleep this one off."

"*All night* with the boys this time, huh? I'm gonna write to the Old Goat and rat on you."

"Don't bother. He'll read it in the obituaries tomorrow. Besides, it wasn't the boys. I was out with the girls this time—a bon voyage party for a couple of friends. But from the shape they were in when I finally left the party, I doubt that their voyage got started. If it did, it sure as hell won't be a *bon* one today; there aren't enough air-sick bags on an entire plane to accommodate the shape they must be in this morning."

"The girls, huh. Martinis, then, I'll bet."

The mere mention of the drink threatened to undo all that the coffee was beginning to accomplish. "Don't you have to study your lines or something?" I asked.

Bogie laughed and laid the script down. The only thing that saved me from a fiendish needling was a knock at the door. It was the makeup man, who entered and quickly set to work. He knew that Bogie didn't like using much makeup and didn't like sitting too long while it was being applied, so he kept up a running monologue—mostly industry gossip—which kept Bogie occupied and gave me a brief respite and time for the coffee to help clear the fuzz from my swirling noggin.

It wasn't long, though, before Bogie said to the makeup man, "Don't slap that powder puff too loud on my face. Pete's got a hangover the size of Rhode Island."

Naturally, the makeup man joined Bogie in the needling, which didn't stop until Bogie judged that he had enough makeup. "Okay, creep," he said, applying the finishing touches to the job himself. "If you work on my mug any longer, you'll have me looking like the leading lady."

After the makeup man left, I began applying Bogie's toupee and blending the makeup into the French lace. On full frontal toupees like Bogie's, the lace covers the forehead down to about an inch or so above the eyebrows. The makeup, if it is applied correctly, makes it impossible to distinguish where the skin ends and the lace begins, even in extreme close-ups. Bogie needled me about my shaky condition while I was putting on the toupee. "Maybe we oughta call in somebody sober to put this damn thing on," he said. "The way you're shaking, you'll have it glued to the back of my neck or something."

"It might be a blessing to everyone involved with this picture if I plastered it across your mouth," I snarled, half-seriously.

When I finished and grabbed my coffee cup again for support, he gave my work a critical inspection in the mirror. "By God, it looks better than it does when you put it on sober!" he said. "You oughta get drunk with the girls more often; you'd make me a matinee idol."

"It wouldn't be worth it," I said.

"But look how handsome I look—and how *sober!*"

I poured us another cup of coffee. We had half an hour before we'd be called to the set, and as usual, this free time was given over to discussion. If there wasn't something in the morning news or in the trades that arrested our attention, we'd talk about the business or about acting. Bogie was convinced that no movie or television actor should go without the experience of performing onstage before live audiences. "Hell, any of them can play summer stock," he said. "And they should; it trims and sharpens an actor's timing, gives him assurance and self-confidence." I once asked him if he ever thought of returning to the theater. "Hell, no," he said. "Fourteen years of that was enough—though I don't regret a moment of it. I probably couldn't make a comeback in the theater, anyway. Besides, I'd never leave the *Santana* and this California weather."

Bogie's pet peeve was actors who claimed not to be actors. The two who did so most often—and Bogie would blow his top every time they did—were Duke Wayne and Gary Cooper. "What the hell's the matter with those guys, anyway?" he'd say. "Someone mentions acting to them, and they dig their toes in the dirt and say, 'Aw, shucks, I ain't no actor.' What the hell are they doing in front of the cameras then? Christ! It took nearly a century in this country for actors to be considered other than whoremongers, and these jerks give the impression that they're *ashamed* of what they do. If they're not actors, they ought to get out of the business."

Bogie didn't think it absolutely necessary for one to have stage experience to become a good actor, but he thought that the experience gave an actor polish, an edge that couldn't be gotten otherwise. "There are fine actors who I don't think have had theater experience," he said. "Gary Cooper's great. So's Clark Gable, Spencer Tracy, Ty Power—a lot of them. And there are those who have extraordinary natural talent and who are underrated, I think. Our ol' friend Killer is a good example." Killer was Bogie's nickname for Errol Flynn, the "lady killer." Flynn and Bogie had been under contract together at Warner Brothers, and they kept in touch. Whenever they got together, which was often, they were like two school chums who had shared the same alma mater. "Some of the broads are damn good, too," Bogie said. "Bette Davis, Katharine Hepburn, Annie Sheridan, and this young one, Audrey Hepburn —she's gonna go far."

Audrey Hepburn was cast in *Sabrina* along with William Holden, and Bogie was very impressed with her work and her potential. Bogie admired Bill Holden's work, too. Columnists and at least one of Bogie's biographers have intimated a rivalry between Bogie and Holden, but none existed to my knowledge. They had no occasion to be close friends, and they were both outspoken individualists, so they may or may not have had professional differences during the filming, but if they did have words, I didn't hear them, and I was on the set every day. I know that Bill Holden stopped in at the bungalow on a couple of occasions to have an afterwork drink with Bogie. Sometimes professional discussions or even slight disagreements on a set are trumpeted by columnists into "feuds"; perhaps that's what happened. I often doubted that I was working on the same picture that columnists were writing about. Particularly Bogie's pictures. On *Sabrina,* he's alleged to have fought with director Billy Wilder because he thought Wilder was giving Audrey Hepburn too much attention, too many close-ups, and the like. He's also supposed to have thrown a tantrum over the script and the script writer. I think that more often than not, the columnists were simply bewildered by Bogie and didn't understand him; I know that his ribbing was often misinterpreted as being serious. It wouldn't have surprised me at all to have read that Bogie and the unit manager had had a serious fight about Bogie's name on the dressing-room door (a rib that I'll detail later). This is not to say that Bogie couldn't be a real pain in the ass, on the set and off. He could and often was. But he seldom got angry unless he had a legitimate complaint, something more substantial than those he's alleged to have had on *Sabrina*.

We were having a second cup of coffee when the phone rang and we were summoned to the set. Bogie grabbed his script, and I followed him out of the bungalow with a Thermos of coffee, the morning paper that he hadn't read yet but would be looking for later, and his makeup box. As we walked along the studio streets toward the sound stage, everyone we passed greeted him. He'd often pause to talk to extras, sound men, carpenters, electricians, or others that he'd worked with. He enjoyed such studio camaraderie; he loved making films, really, and rarely forgot anyone who ever worked with him.

Though we knew that the sound stage wasn't in use at that moment, Bogie and I both looked at the unlit red light fixture above the door before we entered; it's a habit one forms very quickly on a movie lot. The red light above the sound-stage door, as well as those on rolling tripods inside, is lighted whenever a scene is being shot. It's a cardinal sin to open a sound-stage door, through which light and sound can enter, when the red light is lit.

We walked through the door, which opened into a little entryway painted flat black to absorb light and which led to another door opening onto the sound stage. If you've never seen sound stages, it's hard to visualize their immensity. Picture a windowless, empty building designed to keep out all sound and light and large enough to hold an entire city block of three-story buildings; overhead is a labyrinth of wooden catwalks from which are suspended hundreds of spotlights; the floor is strewn with miles of electric cables the diameter of broomsticks. Now if you can picture this cavernous edifice in pitch blackness, and then throw in a few obstacles like electrical panels on wheels, carpenter's sawhorses, backdrop flats, snakelike coils of cables, and the like, you can imagine how difficult it is to make your way into one of those things.

As usual, we had come from direct sunlight into total darkness. All the lights had been killed at the cameraman's request in order to light the set Bogie would be working on. Off in the distance, we could see the lights, but they were about fifty yards away, and there was pitch blackness between us and where we wanted to go.

"I can't see a damn thing," Bogie said.

My eyes grew accustomed to the darkness faster than Bogie's, so I said, "Hang onto my shoulder and follow me."

He did, but as we stumbled around trying to get to the damn set, Bogie said, "This could be disastrous; the blind following the blind is one thing, but asking the blind to follow the drunk is beyond the call of duty."

"You keep smart-mouthing and I'll leave you stranded here to stumble around by yourself," I said.

"Okay, my lips are sealed."

"That'll be a relief."

"But trembling," he added.

Electricians were scurrying around the set. "Kill spot four," one of them called. "That arc on the window is too hot."

Spotlights flicked on and off. Joe Conners, Bogie's longtime stand-in, and the stand-ins for Hepburn and Holden were in the corner of the set and were moving from one place to another, following the pattern as it had been blocked out by the director the night before for the camera setup. Everyone stopped to greet us as we finally found our way into the periphery of light.

A short distance away was Bogie's portable dressing room, which was used for costume changes and for a little privacy between takes. Such rooms were always set up as a convenience because of the great distance between the sound stages and the actors' bungalow dressing rooms. The door to Bogie's said simply: Humphrey Bogart. When the unit manager for *Sabrina* was showing us around the sound stage on the first day of shooting, Bogie had stopped before the door and stared at his name. "What the hell is *this?*" he said to the unit manager.

The guy had never worked with Bogie before, and he was startled by Bogie's apparent displeasure. He looked at the door. "Is something wrong, Mr. Bogart?" he said.

"Is something wrong?" Bogie mocked. "You're damn right there's something wrong! Where the hell's the *mister* on this door? Is this all the respect I'm gonna get in this crappy rattrap? At Warners they always put *Mister Humphrey Bogart* on my portable dressing room. And in big letters, too. Bigger than this. And *neat,* too. Who the hell put my name up here? It looks like some movie mogul scrawled it with a big Crayola."

"No star, either, Bogie," I said.

"Huh?" Bogie said, looking back at the door. "I'll be damned! You're right, Pete." He turned back to the unit manager. "There's no star here, either! They always gave me a big yellow star at Warners—with that sparkly stuff on it. I'm distressed!"

The unit manager had doubtless had to deal with many temperamental stars; he was totally taken in. "Gee, Mr. Bogart," he said, "if I'd known—"

"If?" Bogie interrupted. "If? If a frog had wings, it wouldn't be bumping its ass all the time. How much good does *if* do a frog?"

"I didn't know," the unit manager said. "But I'll have it changed right away."

"Too late for that," Bogie said. "I've already signed the contract. But you better tell Wilder that he'd better give me another few days before he starts shooting; I'll need at least that much time to get mentally up for this picture. You guys have gone and fucked up my ego!"

The unit manager seemed crestfallen until Bogie finally told him it was all a joke. "This business can be a crashing bore if it's taken too seriously," he said. "And another thing, this *mister* stuff is okay in private, but in public, it's Bogie to you, okay?"

From then on, the unit manager was game for anything. He delighted in Bogie's gags, and helped him set up a couple of them.

We went into the portable dressing room and set up for the day's shooting. The wardrobe man came in with the clothes Bogie would be wearing that day. Bogie was very particular about his picture wardrobe, and he checked every detail. Off the set, it was different; almost anything would do as long as it was clean.

By the time Bogie had changed, the assistant director knocked on the door; he had a voice like a hog caller: "Ready for you, Mr. B," he said.

Bogie followed him to the set. The director, Billy Wilder, was scrutinizing the lighting and rechecking the movement he had blocked out. "Okay, genius, I'm here," Bogie said to him. "Where the hell are the rest of the hams?"

"Right here," Bill Holden said, coming onto the set from the opposite direction.

"So where's the broad?" Bogie said.

"She's getting some padding put in her dress," Wilder told him.

"Good," Bogie said. "Every time I squeeze her, her bones nearly cut me in two. How about you, Lover Boy," he added, looking at Holden. Lover Boy was the nickname Bogie had given to him; he seldom called anyone by his true name.

"I can't complain," Holden said.

While they waited for Audrey Hepburn, Wilder briefed them on the scene to be shot. I slipped away toward a cluster of people who were gathered around a hammock that had been set up for Wilder's approval and that would be used in a later scene. It was plastic, and for some reason there was a hole cut out of its center. Several workmen were taking turns testing the

hammock for safety, swinging it, checking to see if anyone could fall through the hole.

I watched them for a minute or so, then heard Bogie
and Bill Holden whispering conspiratorially behind me.
Just as I started to look their way, they grabbed me,
lifted me in the air, and dumped me into the hammock.
My bottom went through the hole, and my legs and
arms stretched helplessly toward the ceiling. I was
stuck. Everyone started laughing, and as Holden began
swinging the hammock high in the air, Bogie went into
a circus-barker routine: "Right this way, ladies and gen-
tlemen! Step right up and get your ticket to the main
attraction on the midway. The mighty midget. All ass
and no forehead!"

Everyone was having a great time until the assistant
director broke up the frivolity. "Mr. Wilder is ready,"
he said.

Work was begun in earnest. Wilder was a meticulous
director, and for the setups that morning he rehearsed
the cast several times and did take after take to get the
scene right. A couple of hours were spent to get just two
or three minutes on film, which wasn't at all unusual.
But by the time they got into the second scene, which
was another long one involving Audrey, Bogie, and
Holden, it was nearly noon. Several of the craftsmen
were beginning to grumble about hunger pains, and
many in the crew were getting restless. After the thir-
teenth take, I stepped in to check Bogie's toupee; the
hot lights made him perspire, and sometimes the spirit
gum would dissolve and soak through the lace, causing
shiny spots. As I touched up his hair, Bogie whispered,
"See if you can get that slave driver to print the next
take, Pete."

"Yeah, Pete," Holden said. "We're starving."

I nodded and left the set. The assistant yelled, "Quiet, everybody!"

The sound man pushed the buzzer to warn people on the sound stage that the camera would be rolling. "Speed!" he yelled.

The scene went perfectly. At the end, Wilder said quietly, "Cut."

There was a long silence. Audrey, Holden, Bogie, and the crew eyed Wilder and awaited his verdict. He sat in his canvas chair, chin cupped in his hands, in deep thought. I moved to his side and bravely broke the silence. "Why the hell don't you print that one?" I said. "It was great. I'm sure they can't do any better."

Wilder looked up at me and stared for a moment. "So *you* think it's good, do you?"

Wilder was an important director, and my audacity was about as subtle as a punch in the eye. He could have banished me from the set and the lot if he'd chosen to. But that didn't occur to me, so I plunged on. "Yeah," I said. "I couldn't have done it better with C. B. De Mille's help."

It was a dumb thing to say, but it was off the top of my head and out of my mouth before I even considered how it sounded. Then it was too late. I guess Wilder was so surprised that I amused rather then angered him. He suddenly smiled and said loudly, "Okay, print the last one. Lunch."

The crew applauded and shouted a few bravos. Wilder walked onto the set and said to Bogie, "We have a new director now. Where the hell did you find *her?*"

Bogie laughed. "Under a rock in Arizona," he said. "Little, but loud."

"Lunch. One hour," the assistant called to the crew.
"Now, Pete!" Bogie shouted to me.

It was our agreed-upon signal that initiated my twice-daily routine, at lunch and again at five thirty in the afternoon. I'd run to the dressing room on the set and close the door behind me. Bogie would follow shortly, closing the door behind him. No one knew what went on behind the closed door. What most of them probably thought went on, didn't. I don't even remember how or why the signal and the haste of the routine started. Maybe just for the hell of it. Anyway, that's the way we did it. What was really going on was that we were breaking a studio rule, like a couple of kids. There was a rigid rule against the use of alcohol on the set. So when Bogie gave his signal, I'd dash in and mix a Scotch and soda, which I'd hand to him when he walked in. We had a whole damn bungalow full of the stuff, and Bogie could have waited the four minutes or so it took to walk from the sound stage to the bungalow, but I always smuggled a bottle onto the set in Bogie's makeup case.

I know that loudmouth helped Bogie relax. One can't just switch off emotions that are built up before the camera. But I think the main reason Bogie wanted it right then and there was because the studio had a rule against it, and he thought it was a stupid rule. Anyway, our action was a mystery to the rest of the actors and crew, and it must have been the cause of much speculation.

On this day, Bogie sat down and took a sip of his drink. "What about that air conditioner for the bungalow?" he said.

I told him that I'd talked to the prop man and people in the maintenance and other departments without luck, so I'd finally got hold of Mr. Don Hartman, the head of the studio.

"You mean you talked to him on the phone?" Bogie asked.

"I had to," I said. "Everyone else gave me nothing but a roomful of feathers, so I went to the top."

"Jesus," he said, "you really get in there where angels fear to tread. What'd he say?"

"That he'd meet us in the bungalow at twelve thirty, if Wilder broke by that time."

"The *head* of the studio is meeting us to discuss a goddamned air conditioner?" Bogie said.

"I don't know why, but that's what he said."

Bogie looked at his watch. "Well, we'd better get over there; it's almost that time now."

As we neared the bungalow, a hurricane struck us—at least that's what it felt like. A great blast of wind hit us from behind, blowing my skirt up over my head and whipping Bogie's toupee so that it flapped down over his face. We dashed for the bungalow, and when we opened the door, there stood Hartman, laughing like hell.

There's always equipment standing around a movie lot or being towed from one place to another. Bogie and I had passed an enormous fan—a powerful wind machine used for storm scenes—a few feet from the bungalow, but we had taken no notice of it. Hartman had ordered the machine brought over from the prop department or wherever they kept the damn things. One of the workmen had stood nearby, switch in hand, and threw it when Hartman gave him the signal from Bogie's dressing-room window. We must have looked funny as hell when we came bursting into the bungalow. My full skirt was flapping around my shoulders and Bogie's toupee was inside out, the hair side hanging over his face, secured only by the lace adhered to his forehead.

Bogie pushed his toupee back on his head and I got my skirt down as Hartman stood looking at us, almost collapsed with laughter. We still didn't know what had hit us. "What the hell's going on?" Bogie asked him. He wasn't mad, just momentarily bewildered.

"Nothing's too good for my actors," Hartman finally managed to say between belly laughs. "Your secretary seemed to think that things were too hot around here for you, so I thought I'd better get you cooled off fast."

Bogie looked out the window at the wind machine and laughed. "I said I wanted something to cool my dressing room, not blow me off the goddamned lot," he said.

"The boys will install an air conditioner this afternoon," Hartman said. He started out the door. "See you later, Bogie," he said, then stopped and looked at me; I looked as though I were wearing a fright wig. He smiled. "And as for you, little lady, if there's anything else you need, just let me know."

Hartman was a man of action, and this one damn near swept us off our feet. No doubt Bogie's reputation as a ribber had preceded him to Paramount, and Hartman got the drop on him. I don't recall whether Bogie ever got even, but I doubt that he'd let such a prank go unchallenged.

This, of course, was not a typical Paramount lunch break. Usually, after a quick drink in the portable dressing room, we'd go to the bungalow, where Bogie always called Betty to report the morning's happenings and to ask about the children; Steve was seven then and Leslie was four. While Bogie was on the phone, I always put out his lunch, which was prepared each morning by May, the Bogart cook, and which almost always consisted of one sandwich, made of tomatoes and cheese; one hard-boiled egg; and a bottle of beer from the kitchenette refrigerator. May always fixed the same kind of lunch for me, which Bogie brought along to the studio with his.

After the wind machine episode, Bogie got on the phone. He talked for a minute or so, then called to me, "Pete, Betty wants to know if you can come by for dinner tonight."

I grimaced and shook my head no.

"She says yeah," he said to Betty on the phone, "but she's got to make an early evening of it. She tied one on last night with the boys."

After he hung up, he said to me, "Now don't get your balls in an uproar. A deal is a deal, sweetheart."

The deal Bogie was talking about was our agreement that I should make appearances in the Bogart home, which I hated. It seemed hypocritical as hell for me to have anything to do with Bogie's home life, and while Bogie agreed with me in principle, he pointed out that it would raise suspicions if I didn't act as an employee of Humphrey Bogart normally would. And so I became more familiar with Betty and the children than I wanted to under the circumstances.

After phoning Betty, Bogie took his lunch, a current news magazine, and the trade papers into one of the dressing rooms and closed the door. We rarely ate our lunch together. Bogie liked his private moments, and he always spent a half-hour eating and catching up on his reading, then took a half-hour nap. He was a great catnapper and could doze off in seconds. As usual, he said, "Knock me up when it's time to go back to the set, Pete."

"It'll have to be about five minutes earlier," I said. "I've got to get this muff of yours straightened out again."

I always went through his fan mail as I ate; usually the fans requested autographed photos of him. I signed them; I had learned to copy his signature exactly. One day he picked up one of the photos, examined the signature, and said, "Good God! Remind me not to leave my checkbook lying around. Your signature looks more like mine than mine does."

The business of my forging Bogie's autograph wasn't at all inconsistent with his philosophy. It had to do with how Bogie perceived himself. He considered himself an actor, not a movie star, and he looked upon autographed photos as "movie star stuff," which he wanted as little to do with as possible. It occurs to me that some who read this may have a treasured autographed picture of him. I don't mean to disillusion anyone, but Bogie wasn't the only actor who had someone on staff autograph photos. And now, with the use of rubber stamps, the practice is even more widespread. I'm sure Bogie did sign a lot of photographs himself, particularly early in his career, but it's not something he liked doing or something he did while I was around.

So I was autographing photos and putting them into envelopes to be sent to the mailroom when the phone rang. It was Bogie's agent, Phil Gersh. "He's taking his nap," I told him.

"Then don't bother him. How do the rushes look?"

"Rushes" are prints of scenes shot that day and "rushed" through the developing process so that the director can see how the scenes look on film. Bogie didn't like looking at the rushes because they usually weren't ready before six o'clock, and Bogie liked to be home by then. He always sent me over to the screening room to look at them for him, and I'd give him a report the next morning.

"The rushes stink," I said to Phil. "Bogie looks more like Audrey's father than her lover."

"Did you tell Bogie that?"

"Of course. He told me I was an insulting bitch and to go fuck myself."

Phil laughed.

"I'll have him call you when he wakes up," I said.

"Don't bother. Just tell him that the Italy deal seems to be coming along fine and that I'll stop by the house tonight and go over a few things with him."

"Okay," I said.

Afternoons on the set were much like the mornings. Bogie had a five-thirty-quitting-time clause in his contract, which he struggled to get because of his early days in Hollywood, when it wasn't uncommon for him to work from five in the morning until eight or ten at night. This is still required of some actors and actresses, especially in television series, which is why such work, though it's not hard physical labor, can be so debilitating; it's not an easy life. But when Bogie got sufficient box-office clout, his agent insisted that except for scenes that required night shooting, Bogie's workday ended at five thirty, and the production company had to give him at least twelve hours' rest before the next day's call.

So at five-thirty, Bogie would retire to his dressing

room, change clothes and have another smash, then go to his bungalow, where I'd take off his toupee and he'd remove his makeup. Sometimes he'd have a couple of people in for a drink or two before heading home.

The *Sabrina* shooting went very smoothly—because it had a very good director in Billy Wilder and because, like Bogie, Audrey Hepburn and Bill Holden were solid professionals who arrived on time, knew their lines, took direction well, gave their best on every take, and were not prima donnas. I've always thought that Bogie was miscast in the film, and it wasn't one of his better ones, but it was certainly one of the easiest and most enjoyable I was involved with.

11

The Santana and Other Pleasures

One can't write a book about Humphrey Bogart without mentioning his racing yawl *Santana,* the only material possession that he really cared about. It would be more accurate to say that the *Santana* possessed him; she was seductive and bewitching, and he loved her in a way that only a man of the sea can comprehend.

Bogie had gone to sea when he joined the navy at eighteen. Prior to that, he had spent summers sailing Canandaigua Lake, one of the Finger Lakes in upstate New York, where his family kept a summer home until they were uprooted by financial reversal. When Bogie decided in the mid-thirties to make a career in films and to settle in Hollywood, one of his first acts was to buy a sleek motor launch, which he renamed *Sluggy* after he married Mayo Methot. During World War II, Bogie volunteered his services and the service of *Sluggy* for civilian patrol, and, flying a United States Coast Guard flag, he cruised the coast looking for enemy submarines, which he never encountered.

About a year or so before he met Bacall, Bogie got rid

of *Sluggy* and bought *Santana;* he bought her from actor Dick Powell, as I recall. She was named for the desert winds, called Santa Ana Winds, that sometimes blow across the southern and central California coast from the east, overpowering the usually prevalent and milder cool western winds that blow in from the Pacific Ocean. The *Santana* was a lovely sailboat, a fifty-five footer, with a galley, a master cabin in the stern, a main cabin amidship, and a small forward cabin. She could sleep eight comfortably, and occasionally did.

The *Santana* was tended by Carl Petersen, a retired fireman and an excellent sailor, whom Bogie kept in his employ from the time he bought the boat until it was sold, after his death. Bogie kept the *Santana* moored in San Pedro harbor, about twenty miles south of Hollywood, and it was there that I first met Captain Pete, as Bogie called him. It was a most memorable—and embarrassing—first meeting.

Bogie had suggested that we spend the weekend on the *Santana* and had gone down to the boat ahead of me because I was working on another picture and couldn't get away until evening. He told me that he didn't have clean sheets for the double bed in the master cabin and asked if I'd bring some down with me. I did. They were gorgeous satin sheets that I thought suitable for the occasion.

The captain was away in town when I came aboard. Bogie and I made the bed—not an easy feat, since it was immobile and one side of it was snug against the bulkhead—and then we went to the clubhouse for dinner and drinks. When we returned to the boat about midnight, high and happy, the captain had retired and we settled in for an amorous night.

Bogie and Me

When it came to love, Bogie was the antithesis of his hard-boiled image. He was very loving, very kind and considerate, and very tender. He wasn't oversexed and a skirt chaser, as many Hollywood men were, and he wasn't the kind who find one-night stands fulfilling. He was a very unselfish lover, and he knew how to make a woman feel like a woman.

I was feeling very much like a woman that night on the boat until, during a romantic interlude, I realized that I had a slight problem. And I told him so. "Wait a minute, Bogie," I said. "I think I've got a problem here."

"What's the matter?" he said.

"You're not gonna believe this, but my foot's caught."

Somehow on the slippery satin sheets I had managed to wedge my foot between the frame of the bed and the bulkhead. I twisted every possible way to get loose, but to no avail. I was really stuck. After I finally convinced him that I wasn't pulling an ill-timed rib, Bogie got up and turned a light on, and we both stared at my leg. I wasn't in pain; it's just that my ankle bones seemed wider than the crevice into which my foot had slipped. Bogie tried to help me get my foot out, but it was no use.

"I don't know how the hell you got your foot in there in the first place!" he said.

"I don't either," I said. "It must have slipped with the goddamned satin sheet."

We tried wedging a corner of the sheet into the crevice, hoping it would be slippery enough for me to ease my foot out. That didn't work either. Then Bogie got down on his hands and knees and inspected the bed, looking for bolts or something to loosen, but there weren't any.

"Christ!" he said. "I've got the only boat in the marina with a built-in broad. I'll have to go get the captain."

"The captain?"

"Do I look like I got a saw on me?" he said, slipping on his dungarees. "I don't even know if we've got a damn saw aboard. Cover up and I'll be right back."

I wrapped the sheet around my body and waited. A few minutes later Bogie returned with the captain in tow. Captain Pete was carrying a keyhole saw, and despite having been awakened at such an early hour, he was good-natured—as he always was. He eyed the problem at hand, and me wrapped in a satin sheet, and he laughed.

"We tried laughter. It doesn't work," Bogie said with mock sarcasm. "What we need is a little muscle. Why don't you use your *head?*"

Bogie and Captain Pete were great friends, and the depth of their friendship was attested to by the number of affectionate names Bogie called him, including Dumb-bum, Squarehead, and half a dozen others. The captain went to work on the board and soon had my foot free. He kissed me on the forehead as Bogie congratulated him on the successful operation. Naturally, the freeing of my foot called for a smash or two of loudmouth. On the *Santana,* anything was an excuse for a celebration.

Bogie was a member of the yacht club in San Pedro —membership came with the rented slip. As an individualist, nonconformist, and sardonic wit, Bogie was considered by some club members to be a little too rowdy, and though there were a few like him with whom he bent elbows at the club bar, he looked with disdain on most of the membership, which he judged to be more than a little too snooty. What really pissed him off were those who looked down their noses at his few harbor friends but who tried to ingratiate themselves with him because of his fame. I was there one day when he got even with one of them.

The guy—I'll call him Mr. Yacht because I've forgotten his true name—was an intolerable snob, a first-class pain in the ass who used to complain to the management because Bogie and I occasionally would visit the clubhouse bar dressed only in bathing suits. Bogie used to tell them, "Look, I can see dressing for *dinner,* but I'll be a son of a bitch if I'm gonna dress for a *drink!*"

Bogie disliked Mr. Yacht for two reasons. He found it incredible that a man could come down to the sea and remain a snob, that a person could be so insensitive as to look out at one of the world's great oceans and not realize how infinitesimal he was in nature's scheme of things. But then Mr. Yacht didn't exactly come down to the sea; that was the other reason Bogie disliked him. Mr. Yacht's magnificent boat was mostly for show. About all he did with it was cruise the harbor, serving his guests vintage wine in crystal glasses.

Mr. Yacht had a summer mansion on the beach, right next to the marina. For years, he threw elegantly lavish patio parties for his society friends. His parties could be seen and heard from the marina's clubhouse, but never in all those years had he invited anyone from the club, which was a sore point among many of the members.

Mr. Yacht finally broke his own snobbish rule—and rued the day.

Bogie and I were aboard the *Santana,* cleaning, waxing, and polishing—it wasn't all drinking, sailing, and frolicking. I used to work my ass off on that boat, but no harder than Bogie did. The *Santana* was always spotless enough to earn the Good Housekeeping Seal. Anyway, we were working when Mr. Yacht asked permission to come aboard. Bogie gave it, and Mr. Yacht said, "I'm giving a little party at my house tonight, Mr. Bogart, and I was wondering if you'd like to attend. It's not black tie; casual—suit coats and dresses will be fine."

"Well, thanks. Yes, I would," Bogie said. "I assume that my secretary here, Pete, is invited, too; I don't like going to parties stag."

"Of course," Mr. Yacht said. "About eightish?"

"Yeah, eightish," Bogie said.

After Mr. Yacht left, I said to Bogie, "Listen, all I brought down here are my jeans, a couple of sweat shirts, and my windbreaker. I'll be damned if I'm gonna go into San Pedro and buy a complete outfit just to—"

"He said *casual* dress, ol' girl," Bogie interrupted.

"Yeah, casual dresses and suit coats."

"Why do you suppose that bastard invited me?"

"To show off to his snooty friends how he hobnobs with movie stars."

"That's what I figure. So that's what we'll give him— a show."

We showed, all right. All of us dressed in bathing suits. I say all of us because Bogie rounded up some of his harbor buddies, all of whom Mr. Yacht would have labeled beach bums. We numbered about a dozen when Bogie knocked on Mr. Yacht's door. Mr. Yacht himself opened it. I stepped in, followed by Bogie, who pulled Mr. Yacht to one side as the other ten or so filed in. We couldn't have found a more motley-looking group; some were even wearing cut-off jeans, and this was about twenty-five years before they became funky-fashionable.

Mr. Yacht stared at the single-file parade of interlopers, and Bogie said, "I knew you wouldn't mind if I brought along a few of our friends. I took a look at your party here from the clubhouse and thought I'd better liven it up before rigor mortis sets in. Where's the bar?"

Before the evening was through, someone in our drunken bunch decided that a bonfire on Mr. Yacht's private stretch of beach would be a warm and cheery addition to the party. They couldn't find any beach wood, so they decided to use whatever was at hand. I was on the patio when the fire was started, but when we gathered around it to sing, I saw that at least two chairs from Mr. Yacht's house had been sacrificed—French provincial, I think. It was hard to tell because they had been broken into so many pieces and were burning when I saw them. I don't know whose idea it was to use the chairs, but Bogie certainly did nothing to discourage it.

We were far from remorseful while we were having breakfast aboard the *Santana* the following morning. "You realize," I said to Bogie, "that Mr. Yacht will never speak to you again."

Bogie considered my remark for a moment. "Do you think you could get him to put that in writing?" he said.

I was never aboard the *Sluggy*. Mayo was a good sailor and so was usually aboard whenever Bogie was. But it was different with the *Santana*. Bogie said that

Betty found sailing a bore; she had apparently tried to get interested in it when they were first married, but she was far less enthusiastic about the rugged sport than Bogie and so left the sea to him. After Bogie's death, the *Santana* was sold, to someone in San Francisco, I believe. It's been a long time since then and she's probably no longer in service, but I hope she is—I like to think so.

I spent a good deal of time aboard *Santana,* at her slip in San Pedro Harbor and on weekend trips to Santa Catalina Island, which is about thirty miles from the mainland and which took about four hours to sail, depending upon the weather. Catalina, as it's called, is an unspoiled island that once belonged to the Wrigley family (of chewing-gum fame). Its only town, Avalon, is a tourist attraction. At that time, I doubt that over a hundred people lived on the island year-round, but hundreds of people were attracted to it in summer. It has small shops, a bank, a hotel, a casino, and a dance pavilion that still attracts big-name bands. We rarely went into Avalon, though. We used to moor at Cherry Cove, a marvelous shelter on the bay side of the island, with crystal-clear water for swimming and a small strip of beach. Cherry Cove was the primary anchorage for many of the boats that came over from the mainland.

Usually just the three of us—Bogie and me and Captain Petersen—made the trip to Catalina. Captain Pete liked having me along because I loved to cook and relieved him of that duty whenever I was aboard. He particularly liked my chili and beans, which was Bogie's favorite and which he usually had me make a big batch of during our weekend voyages. I always cooked the beans in soda water first to neutralize the gas. Bogie thought this a stroke of genius and bragged indelicately to visitors that the *Santana's* menu featured my "fart-less" chili.

Many movie people sailed with Bogie, such as Errol Flynn, David Niven, and Frank Sinatra, but naturally I wasn't invited on those occasions because such outings were social and not conducive to the low profile of our affair. We did meet people at Cherry Cove, though. Errol Flynn was often there with his own boat, *Zaca*, and sometimes we'd be joined by someone who was visiting Avalon. Winstead "Doodles" Weaver used to visit the boat often. Doodles gained fame as an entertainer with the Spike Jones orchestra and with zany hits like "Feetlebaum," his famous horse-race record.

Once when Doodles was aboard, we spent the afternoon sunning and talking and drinking. By sundown, we were all pretty well steeped in Scotch and soda and getting hungry. Captain Peterson always set out lobster traps whenever we anchored in Cherry Cove, and it was decided that fresh lobster and a bottle of white wine were exactly what we needed to top off the evening. While Captain Pete prepared to board the dinghy to check the traps, Doodles and Bogie made a bet as to the number of lobsters, if any, he had caught. Doodles finally decided to check the traps personally; there was a hundred-dollar bet at stake.

Before we realized his intentions, Doodles scampered up the main mast like a monkey. He was feeling pretty high, but he could climb like hell. He had decided to dive off the mast rather than over the side and swim to the traps.

"Doodles! You crazy idiot!" Bogie said when he saw what Doodles was doing. "Get the hell off my mast. If you scratch it, you're gonna paint it!"

"I'm barefoot," Doodles said.

"Yeah? Well, you got toenails!"

By this time, Doodles had climbed above the first cross-rig to the second, which was probably about forty feet above the deck. The boat was listing away from the direction Doodles would dive; he'd have to dive out at least ten feet or so in order to clear the side.

Bogie was alarmed, but he tried to sound casual and calm. "C'mon down from there, Doodles. You could fall and kill yourself, for Christ's sake! You're drunk."

"Listen, Bogie," Doodles said, swaying back and forth on the mast, "just because you're drunk doesn't mean that everyone else in the world is drunk, you know."

"I'm the captain of this vessel, and I'm ordering you down from there immediately!"

"Oh. Well, aye, aye, captain," Doodles said. He waited for the *Santana* to list toward the lobster traps, then dove off.

He cleared the side by six feet, and the thrust of his push against the mast left the *Santana* rocking back and forth like a cork. The water was about thirty feet deep where we were anchored, so there was little chance of his hitting bottom, but when he didn't surface for a couple of minutes, we all panicked, and Captain Pete manned the dinghy and began rowing out toward where he had dived. Finally, though, Doodles surfaced near one of the traps. "There's one in this one," he called.

When he finally saw that Doodles was okay, Bogie's fear for him turned to anger. "Doodles, you dumb bastard! You could've—"

"Don't worry about me," Doodles interrupted, "My father built this ocean." Then he ducked beneath the surface again, swimming toward the next lobster trap. He had no trouble distinguishing Bogie's traps from others anchored in the cove; trapping lobsters was illegal in those waters, so rather than use the usual kind of buoy to mark the traps, Captain Pete marked ours by tying empty Scotch bottles to the lines.

When Doodles finally climbed back aboard, Bogie ranted and raved at him for about five minutes; he had really feared for Doodles's life. Meanwhile, Doodles sat with a fresh Scotch and soda in his hand and a smile on his face, just listening. And when Bogie's anger was finally spent, Doodles said, "Don't try to change the subject, Bogie. You lost the bet. You owe me a quick hundred!"

Bogie had to laugh.

"Pay up," Doodles said, holding his palm out.

"Will you promise not to play 'Feetlebaum' again if I do?" Bogie said.

"Feetlebaum" was the rage that year, and every time it was played on the radio, Doodles would turn it up full volume and blast it at the boats on the bay.

"You're asking me to deprive music lovers of my classic?" Doodles said.

"Yeah."

"That's a lot to ask for a lousy C note—which you owe me anyway," Doodles said, "but you just happen to have caught me in a conciliatory mood, so—"

"Drunk, you mean," Bogie interrupted.

"Conciliatory," Doodles repeated, "which you in your inebriated state probably can't even pronounce.

Now, I will promise not to aim my radio at your vessel before sunrise."

"Well, that's better than nothing."

"Okay. Pay up."

"I don't have any cash with me."

"I'll take a check."

"I don't carry my checkbook with me."

"Then get me paper and a pencil," Doodles said. "I'll have to put a lien on the *Santana.*"

By then, Captain Pete had returned with three lobster tails, and as I was heading down to the galley to cook them, Bogie was threatening to throw Doodles overboard and make a run toward Mexican waters to avoid paying the debt; Doodles was threatening to sing several choruses of "Feetlebaum."

Those were great times. I haven't seen Doodles Weaver since—except on television—but I understand that he's living in Burbank, collecting classic automobiles, fishing, and still doing occasional movies and television commercials.

Captain Pete's penchant for poaching lobsters at Cherry Cove was the cause of another incident, too. One day the owner of a boat anchored nearby rowed his dinghy to the *Santana* and climbed aboard. He accused Captain Pete of stealing lobsters from his traps. Bogie was incensed by the accusation and ordered the man off his boat. The man refused to go unless he was promised that no one aboard the *Santana* would raid his traps again. Bogie said, "Oh, you're not goin', huh?" He turned to Captain Pete and someone else who was aboard at the time—I don't remember who—and said, "Get this son of a bitch off my boat!" Captain Pete and the other man picked the intruder up and threw him overboard. The man swam to his dinghy and rowed away, shouting obscenities when he was a safe distance from the *Santana*.

Bogie's yawl wasn't our only rendezvous besides my home in Burbank. On a few occasions, we stayed at the Beverly Hills Hotel, whose secluded bungalows were sometimes the hideout for Howard Hughes. We didn't stay there often, though, because Bogie didn't trust room service and refused to call them; this was at a time when *Confidential* magazine's intimate revelations were scaring hell out of many Hollywood celebrities. Hughes used to have his food left in the crotch of a tree outside his bungalow, where he'd sneak out to get it when no one was in sight. We didn't think of that.

One night we were on the set at Paramount when one of the studio policemen came around and informed Bogie that torrential rains had flooded all the access roads to his Holmby Hills home. Bogie called Betty and told her that he'd dine in town and that if the rain didn't let up, he'd take a room at a hotel. Meanwhile, I learned that the San Fernando Valley streets were impassable, too, so we decided to go to the Beverly Hills Hotel, which we could reach by taking the hilly, back-street route.

Bogie left his car at the studio, and I drove. The water was over our hubcaps in some areas, and my brakes were almost useless by the time we arrived, but we made it safely. We decided to stop in at the hotel's Polo Lounge for a drink before Bogie registered. Before we could ask for a table, Errol Flynn spotted us and asked us to join him at his table. Killer was sitting with his latest youthful flame, a seventeen-year-old who had just been put under contract at one of the major studios.

Flynn introduced her to us and told us that she had won a beauty contest in Europe. When Bogie heard that, he naturally introduced me to her as "Miss Arizona of Nineteen Thousand."

We talked for a while. Flynn did most of the talking, telling us his young mistress's entire life story, which, owing to her youth, wasn't long. Bogie needled him about cradle snatching, and Flynn just flashed that dazzling smile of his; he was a charmer.

"One of these days," Bogie said, "You're gonna learn your lesson with all this San Quentin Quail."

Flynn just laughed. "God hates a coward," he said.

Bogie asked him where he was keeping his boat; apparently Bogie had noticed that it wasn't in its customary slip.

"Oh, Uncle Sam borrowed it for a while," Flynn said. "Until I catch up on a few payments I owe him."

"Wait a minute," Bogie said. "You mean the IRS took your *boat?*"

"Impounded it for the time being," Flynn said.

"Is nothing *sacred* to those sons-a-bitches? They might just as well put a man in debtors' prison as take his boat!"

"I'll drink to that," Flynn said.

"You're welcome aboard the *Santana* anytime. You know that."

"Yeah, I know that."

Bogie grew solemn. The idea that Flynn's boat had been taken away from him was depressing. Finally he held up his glass in toast. "Here's to you, and here's to your boat. I hope the hell you get it back soon," he said.

"By God, I'll drink a double to that," Flynn said.

We talked for a while longer, then Bogie excused

himself to see about getting a bungalow. "Probably a lot of others stranded in town, too," he said. "I don't want to be left high and wet." He returned shortly with a key. We had another round of drinks; then Flynn borrowed Bogie's bungalow for a while.

"Leave the key at the desk," Bogie said. "Pete and I will be upstairs at the restaurant getting something to eat. In fact, c'mon up and join us. What you have in mind ought to be finished before we're even through with our soup."

Flynn laughed. "We'll see," he said.

We took the elevator up to the restaurant, where Bogie borrowed a tie from the maitre d' to get in. In those days, most good restaurants wouldn't let men in without one, no matter who they were, and women in slacks were refused entrance, too. Romanoff's had the same policy; Bogie and Mike Romanoff fought for months until Mike finally gave up in disgust. Bogie hated to wear ties, and he was the only man I ever saw get into Romanoff's without one.

After dinner, Bogie checked with the desk for his key. Flynn hadn't returned it; in fact, that was the last we saw of Killer or the key, so Bogie finally took another bungalow. I think Flynn kept the bungalow as a joke. "That'll teach me to wisecrack about his sexual prowess," Bogie said.

When we were almost finished shooting *Sabrina,* Phil Gersh called again and said that he had firmed up the "Italy agreement," which I learned was a contract for Bogie to star opposite Ava Gardner in *The Barefoot Contessa,* to be filmed on location in Italy. Since I was a party to the contract, Bogie drove me over to his place, where Phil was to meet us later.

Bogie had a nice two-story white colonial house—a mansion, really—on Mapleton Drive just off Sunset in Holmby Hills. Bing Crosby and Judy Garland were among his celebrity neighbors. I had been to his place many times and had given his children, Leslie and Steve, their first haircuts; I continued to cut Stephen's hair until he was no longer afraid of barbers. The first time I had seen the Holmby Hills house, after the Bogarts moved from their Benedict Canyon place, I knew that Bogie was a little embarrassed about its enormity and location—he was still worried about "going Hollywood." So, of course, I needled him.

"You couldn't find anything larger, huh?" I said.

"Goddamn snakes!" Bogie said. "They cost me a fortune. There were snakes in Benedict Canyon, and Betty was afraid the baby might get bit; moved me right out to Mapleton Drive."

"She was right," I said. "This is a much nicer place and a much better location."

"Sure," Bogie said. "Take her side. You broads are all alike; the more you get, the more you want. Look at this joint. I don't even know how many rooms we've got. What have we got, twenty? All those rooms, and furniture you can't even use."

His reference to the furniture was an exaggeration. Betty had bought a coffee table with a beautiful Italian marble top, which I had admired. Bogie had snarled at me and the table when I admired it. He hated that table. Italian marble is very porous, and the first time Bogie set a drink on it, Betty chewed him out and gave him a lecture on marble. "Christ!" Bogie said. "Every time I look up, she's shoving a coaster at me. What the hell good's a table you can't even set a goddamned drink on? I'm gonna cover the damn thing with plywood one of these days to make it serviceable. You broads are all alike with your houses and your furniture. I could put a down payment on an entire foreign country for the dough this joint set me back, and I can't even set my drink down without having to go find one of those little fucking coasters! It's a wonder she didn't get marble coasters, too."

When we arrived at the house to meet Phil Gersh, Bogie's butler, Russel, let us in. Betty hurried across the marble floor of the closed-in lanai, which connected the entranceway to the den. She said hello to me and kissed Bogie. "Darling," she said, "there are some drama students from UCLA in the den. They've been waiting for you."

She took his arm and opened the door to the Butternut Room, as it was called. It was an oak-paneled room, large, comfortable, and homey. It had high windows to the ceiling that overlooked the garden and pool below. There were many pictures on the walls, mostly family portraits and a large one of the *Santana*. One wall was covered with books, and there was an alcove with a bar and a fireplace where the walls were covered with photos of friends and a couple of silver trophies—one of them, a racing trophy, had been won by the *Santana*. Across from the alcove were two long couches facing one another, an occasional chair, and several tables.

The alcove, with its bar, was Bogie's favorite spot. That was where he usually sat at the "freeloader" gatherings, the afternoon smashes he held for friends, including members of the Holmby Hills Rat Pack, as they were known to themselves, of which Bogie was the founder and which Frank Sinatra kept going for a while after Bogie's death. Bogie was forever ordering liquor for the alcove bar, claiming that he drank very little of it. "Those freeloaders are the ones who are doing all the drinking and making free phone calls," he always said.

Bogie spoke with deprecation about the freeloaders, but of course they weren't that. And the afternoon cocktail hour with them was the highlight of his day. He was a most gracious host, and he loved entertaining in his home. He wasn't one for throwing big parties, except at Christmastime; he preferred intimate gatherings of his close friends. The freeloader meetings were continued even when he became deathly ill and had to be brought downstairs in a wheelchair.

Bogie's three boxer dogs came galloping across the entryway as Betty opened the door to the Butternut Room. Inside, the five drama students stood up to greet Bogie, but they had to wait another moment or two because the dogs couldn't be denied Bogie's attention. The older of the three dogs was one of a pair given to the Bogarts by author Louis Bromfield. Bogie loved those dogs, but his neighbors didn't. The dogs had the audacity to bark (aloud!) in fashionable Holmby Hills.

The five drama students were still standing when Bogie finally entered the room. They were in their late teens and early twenties, three boys and two girls. "Keep your seats," Bogie said, heading towards the bar. "Who wants a drink?"

"Oh, we don't drink, Mr. Bogart," one of them said.

Bogie got three glasses from the shelf and reached for the Scotch. "You don't drink? I don't understand you sons-a-bitches. What are you, a bunch of fags or something?" He poured the Scotch and reached for the soda, looking up as he did so. "Oh," he added, "I see you're well supplied with Cokes."

Bogie's calling the students sons-a-bitches and questioning their sexuality may seem strange. But in the context of the meeting, it was vintage Bogart. In the brief time he spent with them, the substance of his remarks underscored his rather shocking—to them, at least—opening lines. They were in the big, sumptuous mansion of a movie star and had jumped to their feet, practically standing at attention, when he entered the room. This didn't pass unnoticed, and Bogie's opening lines were calculated to shock their feet back to the ground—to the gutter, in fact. He wanted it understood that they were dealing with a flesh-and-blood person, not a star—someone like them who was lucky enough to be making a good living doing what he wanted to do.

"So you wanna talk shop, huh?" he said. "Well, I can't talk with a dry throat." He squirted soda into the glasses and handed two of them to me; I handed one to Betty. Bogie took a sip of loudmouth, then said, "Okay, fire away."

Bogie liked young people and was always ready to help them if he could. Producers and directors knew this, and they often referred small groups like the one from UCLA to him. He let them do a lot of the talking, listening to their views on acting. Sometimes he'd shoot a glance that would bring the speaker stammering to a stop. He wasn't reluctant to tell them when he thought they were wrong—or when they were right. At this meeting, he wanted to talk acting, but he knew they had to get the "movie star" questions out of their systems first, so he was tolerant.

"How does one break into movies?" one of them asked, "and which is more important, talent or looks?"

"You've gotta have some talent, or you'll be a flash in the pan. Looks help. Luck's important, too—being in the right place at the right time. That isn't all luck, either; it implies activity, knocking on doors and learning one's craft so that when the doors open, you've got more to show than the hat in your hand. If you're a broad, you might get lucky just sitting on a stool in a drugstore or on the beach in a bikini, but you'd better have something inside to back up what's outside."

"Do you consider Katharine Hepburn a good actress?"

"In my opinion, they don't make 'em any better. She's one in a million."

"How did it feel to win the Academy Award after all those years?"

"I should have accepted it lying down. I think half my career has been spent in a horizontal position—having been beaten up, shot, stabbed, or all three at once. But kidding aside, it felt good. It's a tribute from a lot of professionals who take our business seriously. It doesn't make anyone the best of anything, though. As far as I'm concerned, all the actors would have to play the same part in the same film for any kind of logical comparison. Even then, it wouldn't mean much. Acting's an art, not a science. You can't measure it, and you sure as hell can't measure the portrayal of one part against the portrayal of a completely different part. My Oscar was a tribute from people in the industry who decided that it was my turn to be recognized for whatever I've contributed to the industry. It's nothing more than that, but that's honor enough."

"Who's the best film director?"

"I've only worked with a handful, but like best actor, there's no such animal as best director. I've only worked with a couple of them that I don't think deserved the title; the rest are all good. If you want my personal favorite, I'd say John Huston. I don't know what a genius is—except maybe for Einstein—but if someone asked me to define *genius,* I'd point to Huston and let them try to figure the crazy bastard out."

Questions were asked about acting theory, but Bogie claimed no knowledge of it. He stressed learning the basics of the craft so that it becomes second nature, particularly stagecraft. "Then don't act," he told them. "Once you've mastered the craft to the best of your ability, then just think it and you'll be it."

Kathy, Bogie's "real" executive secretary, interrupted the meeting to announce that Phil Gersh had arrived. Kathy was an attractive, middle-aged woman with graying hair; she had been with Bogie for many years. Kathy's father had been a friend of Bogie's, and Bogie had promised her father that he would look after her when her father died. He kept his promise.

Bogie apologized to the students for having to break up the meeting. "My parting advice is this," he said. "If you're lucky enough to get a big break—that big part —grab it, but hold off on the big house and the big cars or you'll be up to your ass in studio brass the rest of your life. The only point in making big money is so that you can tell some big shot to go to hell."

When the students left, Bogie and Phil went into the den to discuss business. I went upstairs with Betty to see if we could coax Stevie to sit still long enough for me to trim his hair. "He's still scared stiff of barbers," Betty said, "and if he doesn't have another haircut soon, I'll have to start braiding it."

Except when I could be useful to her, Betty was usually very cool towards me. I've always suspected that she knew—or at least had suspicions—about my relationship with Bogie. But Bogie was positive that she didn't know. Naturally Bogie and I discussed the possibility of her knowing, particularly when Betty began treating me as she would household help. In a crowd, I'd be the last one she'd greet—if at all. And Bogie admitted that Betty had questioned him about me a few times, suggesting that he seemed a little too friendly to me or questioning my going on trips with him. But Bogie had told her he had to have someone work with him, and the fact that I could do his hair, too —which was vital to his public appearances—was to his advantage.

Anyway, for whatever reason, Betty was always a little condescending towards me. Perhaps it was owing to my own attitude towards her. I don't know. From my point of view, I had always considered her an opportunistic interloper, and when I got to know her better, I amended my opinion. I considered her a pretentious, opportunistic interloper.

In truth, we never had cross words, but under the circumstances I didn't like being around her or the Bogart household. I went as a special favor to Bogie, though. As he frequently pointed out to me whenever I complained, we were working together and it was only natural that I should visit his place on business or attend an occasional social function. Not to have done so would have looked very suspicious. So I went to the house, more or less under duress. And of course Bogie often devised necessities for my putting in an appearance, and we occasionally battled about that.

Betty managed to corral Stevie long enough for me to shear his locks, then Leslie insisted on attention too, so I bobbed her hair. We were cleaning up the barbering when Bogie came in to say good night to the children. Then he told Betty and me to join him in the den.

Russel, the butler, had set out a tray of hors d'oeuvres and was mixing drinks when we got downstairs. Bogie smiled at Phil. "Should we let them in on the latest, Junior?" he said.

"I guess there's no hiding it from them," Phil said.

"Well," Bogie said, "you girls ready to go to Italy?"

I was delighted, but Betty shot me a sidelong glance. I guess Bogie saw it, too, for he quickly added, "Pete, you can huddle with Phil here on what he's worked out for you on the contract. I think he got you a good deal."

Betty didn't say anything, but I got the impression that she wasn't terribly thrilled about my being a part of Bogie's studio equipment. Bogie was to report to Rome January 4, 1954; principal photography would begin on the eleventh. We all drank a toast to *The Barefoot Contessa* and to Rome before Phil had to leave for another appointment. Bogie, Betty, and I had another drink before going in to dinner.

After dinner, Bogie walked me to the car and kissed me good night. "Looks like we may have a little time together in Europe," he said.

"Oh, sure," I said. "Just Bogie and me, and Baby makes three."

"Maybe not for a little while."

"How do you figure that?" I said.

"Betty's thinking of coming over after the picture starts shooting."

"I see. Look, from now on, let me get with Phil in his office on these contracts, will you? I know I've got to put in appearances, but let's not go out of our way to make them necessary, okay? Not on *every* contract, anyway. These little domestic scenes aren't easy to handle, you know."

"Yeah," Bogie said. "I know."

12

Mr. Buchwald and the French Grand Master

Sabrina was finished ahead of schedule, so we had a brief vacation over the Christmas holidays before Bogie and I left for Europe. Since *The Barefoot Contessa* shooting would take at least three months, Betty decided that rather than leave the children for that length of time, she'd stay behind and join Bogie in Italy the following month.

I've forgotten the reason, but rather than going directly to Rome, Bogie decided to go first to Paris, where we'd spend a few days; perhaps it was part of a PR push for *Sabrina.* Since our flight to Paris would originate from the East Coast, we flew first to New York, where we spent a day and a night. We took rooms at the St. Regis and dined on oysters at 21; it was unthinkable for Bogie to pass through New York without stopping there. Then we took an all-night flight to Paris. In those days, trans-Atlantic flights took ten hours.

Paris was just awakening when we touched down at Orly Airport, but the press was out in full force. Flashbulbs popped as we descended the ramp, and we were met by a large company of airport officials, who eased our way through customs and then on to Orly's VIP lounge, where a reception party had been arranged. On our way to customs, we met columnist and humorist Art Buchwald, who was an American correspondent in France then. Buchwald asked Bogie what he was doing in Paris and how long he'd be staying. Bogie told him he had stopped for a brief rest before starting another picture—and to play a game of chess. Bogie had mentioned something to me about a chess game, but I never did figure out how it was set up or why. Buchwald said he'd drop in at the lounge before the reception was over.

When we got to the VIP lounge, it was packed to capacity with press people, and a chess board had been set up at a small table. A French chess grand master, whose name I don't recall and who was to play Bogie, was already seated at the table, waiting.

"Jesus!" Bogie said. "I didn't know they were going to have this game the moment I stepped off the damn plane. I guess these Frenchmen want to get me before I have a chance to blow town."

Bogie looked at his opponent, nodded and smiled, then turned to me and said, "I'm a little beat from that flight, but as soon as I have a smash of loudmouth, I'll give this guy a run for his money."

He sat down at the chess table. The grand master smiled and bowed without rising. He had a smug attitude and expression that irritated hell out of me; it seemed he thought he had Bogie beat before the game had even begun. I don't know how much of this may have been an act on the Frenchman's part—psychology plays an important part in chess, as anyone who has watched or read about international chess competition knows—but if the Frenchman's haughtiness was an act, he was a damned good actor. If I had sat down to play him, my first move would have been to hit him with my purse. But it didn't seem to faze Bogie, who was known in his own chess circles for his coolness under pressure. He had taken lessons from the American grand master Herman Steiner, who was chess editor for the Los Angeles *Times* in those days and gave lessons to many movie-colony people. Steiner was once quoted as saying that Bogie was the best of his Hollywood students and that the iciness he brought to his chillingly real gangster portrayals on screen was really part of his competitive nature and the reason he was such a good chess player.

I don't know who won the draw for white and made the first move, but only a couple of moves had been made when someone brought Bogie a Scotch and soda. Bogie took a long drink of it, then turned his attention back to the board. Meanwhile, the grand master seemed surprised at Bogie's action. Even taking the time difference into account—our bodies were still running on Manhattan time, where it was late at night rather than early morning—Scotch is not something to be sipped during a serious chess match, which requires a clear mind and enormous concentration. The grand master seemed more confident than ever—if that was possible—at the promise of victory.

As the game progressed, it became evident to the spectators that Bogie was no pushover. By mid-game, he was on his second glass of loudmouth, though he took only a sip of it, and the Frenchman was beginning to perspire. Bogie grew calmer; he had control of the board and had his opponent's forces in such a cramped position that, as Bogie told me later, the Frenchman began a move to exchange pieces and force a draw.

I don't know much about chess, but I knew when the end came. The Frenchman made a move, then, remaining bolt upright, his face distraught, he hovered over the board as though someone had a gun trained on him. Bogie regarded the move for only a few seconds, then made a countermove and sat back, totally relaxed, looking away from his opponent and the board for the first time. The Frenchman seemed horrified. To me, chess is just another game, but not to chess enthusiasts; strong men have been known to crack mentally and physically during competition, and I have no doubt that the prospect of losing to a movie star was cause for dismay to the grand master. The Frenchman studied the board in disbelief for several minutes, then, seeing that his position was untenable, he stood up, bowed to Bogie in resignation, and strode from the room without a word. Bogie had won.

Amid a smattering of applause, Bogie said, "How do you like that? He wouldn't even wait around to share a bottle of champagne with me. Get us a magnum of that stuff, Pete, and we'll drink a toast to my tutors: Mike Romanoff and Herman Steiner." Romanoff got top billing because he was the one with whom Bogie most often played and from whom he had learned the most in competition. Romanoff beat Bogie more often than not; he could have been a nationally ranked player had he chosen. For Mike and Bogie both, chess was just a hobby, but a very serious one. Bogie often said that he liked chess because there was no luck in it; it was all skill and concentration.

After the game, news people bombarded Bogie with questions about his playing skill. Bogie had the champagne passed around and thoroughly enjoyed the news session, which was refreshing; for once, people were interested in Bogart the man, not the movie star.

When the reception ended, we left for our hotel, the Ritz, in the heart of Paris. Again we were given the VIP treatment. I was astonished at how popular Bogie was with the Parisians. We were shown to our suites, and Bogie decided to take a short nap. He hadn't slept on the airplane as much as he usually did, and I'm sure that the chess game had taken a lot out of him.

I wasn't at all tired, so I went to my suite to unpack and bathe. My rooms were lovely, overlooking the place Vendôme. I stood at the window for a while; I never cease to marvel at the beauty of Paris. Then I began unpacking and preparing my bath. By this time, though, the switchboard had begun channeling all Bogie's calls to me. The phone didn't stop ringing. There were requests for photographs, autographs, appointments, interviews. I got calls from media people, friends, fans, hotel guests, and many calls in French, which I neither speak nor understand. It seemed that everyone in Paris was calling Bogie. I'd no sooner drop the phone onto its cradle than it would ring again. Finally I shut the phone off, soaked in the tub for about half an hour, took a brief rest, then wrote a short letter to Walter, asking him to visit me in Rome if he could possibly manage it.

Then I was lured to the window again. It was a beautiful sunny day, with a slight chill in the air. I was rested and restless and wanted to get out. It was almost time for another press conference, and besides, I knew that

Mr. Buchwald and the French Grand Master

Bogie didn't want to sleep too long or he'd have trouble sleeping that night. It was imperative that he get used to European time. As any traveler knows, it's not easy adjusting one's inner time clock, and when one has to appear fresh before harsh lights and a camera, trying to get day and night turned around takes more than a little adapting. I called Bogie's suite. He picked up the phone on the fourth ring.

"It's me," I said.

"Yeah, hello, Pete. I knew it was you. I was just shaving. What's up?"

"You've got a press conference in about an hour," I said, "and I'm getting antsy. You feel like being a tourist afterward?"

"Hell yes," Bogie said. "Gay Paree and like that. Order some ice sent up here, will you? Then come on over. I've had all the rest I need."

I ordered the ice and finished dressing. The waiter was just leaving when I arrived. Bogie was mixing two tall drinks, and he handed me one as I walked in. "What do the appointments look like?" he asked.

"There's a press conference. A Mr. Moore's in the lobby now, waiting to take us there. He says it's being held just around the corner from the hotel. Other than that, I've only committed to two: Art Buchwald's dinner invitation for tonight and a meeting with General Gunther and a tour of the American base tomorrow."

"Good. Let's not commit to anything else, huh? We've gotta get to Rome, and we can't leave without seeing Paris, right?"

"Right. I should cut your hair, too. It's getting awfully unmanageable."

"To hell with it," Bogie said. "I don't want to do it on

Paris time. We'll use one of my shaggy muffs until we get to Rome."

The press conference was a good one, with lots of questions about the morning's chess game. It was a refreshing change from all the usual questions, and Bogie enjoyed himself. Near the end of the conference, someone asked who I was. I cringed. I didn't think the French press would back off from Bogie's "mistress" answer as the Americans did, but fortunately Bogie wasn't in a perverse mood.

"That's Pete," he said, "my executive secretary. She's the fastest typist in all of California and can take dictation faster than anyone can talk."

I thought, what the hell is this?

"That reminds me, Pete. Take down a few things for me."

It had to be another rib. I got a pencil and a note pad from my bag, and Bogie began rattling off everything he could think of besides the Declaration of Independence. I went along with it, making meaningless hieroglyphics until he finally wound down. Then the inevitable happened. Before I could hurriedly stick the damn pad and pencil back in my purse, he got that fiendish grin on his face that I knew meant trouble.

"Oh, wait a minute, Pete. I think I left something out of that first part. Read it back to me."

I stalled by rifling back through the pages of meaningless squiggles, wondering how or if he was going to let me off the hook. But Bogie waited patiently, as the press people stood by waiting and watching me. Then Art Buchwald walked in, mercifully diverting everyone's attention. I had only met Mr. Buchwald that morning at the airport, but his entrance at that moment earned my profound gratitude and respect; he had saved me from making a complete ass of myself.

That night at dinner Bogie told Buchwald about the rib, which Bogie still thought was hilarious. Buchwald took us to one of the finest restaurants in Paris—in Europe, for that matter—Tour d'Argent, known for its pressed duck, each of which has been assigned a number since the first was served in 1890. Bogie couldn't get over the absurdity of numbering ducks, let alone eating a numbered duck.

Several preliminary dishes were served, each with a different and wonderful wine, and the combination of alcohol and travel fatigue soon reduced Bogie and me to a splendid giddiness. This must have puzzled Mr. Buchwald, but, gentleman and perfect host that he was, he tactfully overlooked it. Mr. Buchwald is a charming and amusing man, and Bogie liked him. And while the two of them were talking, I was drawn to the duck press. I was a chef at heart even then, and in my inebriated state, I simply seized the press and began pressing every duck within reach. Buchwald spotted me before the management could intervene; he was well known and one of the famous restaurant's most frequent patrons, which is probably the only reason I wasn't tossed out of the place on my can.

While Bogie roared with laughter—an act that brought my wayward ways to the attention of even more people—Buchwald tactfully approached me and said, "Hmmmm. Experimenting, huh? How's it going, Pete?"

"Great," I said, rather thick-tongued, "jus' great!"

"Un-huh. Well, you seem to have mastered the technique. Don't you think we ought to return to the table? Our duck is being served now."

We returned to our table and ate our duck, which was delectable. I was only vaguely aware of the icy Gallic stares that the Tour d'Argent personnel—and not a few of the patrons—were giving me for having seized the duck press.

After coffee and Drambuie, Mr. Buchwald paid the check, and as we were leaving, the captain bowed low and said to me, "I hope Madam has enjoyed herself." He didn't mean it, of course; he would have enjoyed chaining me to a sink to wash mountains of dishes as penance for my unthinkable behavior. Then he turned to Bogie: "Did you enjoy the view, Monsieur?"

Bogie grinned. "Tell him about the view, Pete."

The view had been magnificent. Buchwald's table was one of the best in the house, before a window overlooking the Seine and a wonderful view of Notre Dame. Ordinarily I would have told the captain what he expected to hear, but Bogie's cue called for a rib, not the truth; besides, the captain had called me madam instead of mademoiselle, and I wasn't that old.

"Hell, those old buildings all look alike to me," I said to the startled captain.

Buchwald, who as host felt responsible for us and whose welcome at Tour d'Argent may well have been worn dangerously thin by my seizure of the duck press, hurried us out of the famous restaurant. At the car, we thanked him and let him off the hook when he offered to take us on a tour of the night spots. He may have been relieved to be rid of us that night, but maybe not;

Mr. Buchwald and the French Grand Master

Mr. Buchwald has a wonderful appreciation of the absurd. I haven't seen him since, but I've often wondered whether our escapade resulted in his being banished to a table by the Tour d'Argent scullery door.

Mr. Buchwald gave us the names of several places worth seeing, which we promptly forgot in our tipsy state, so we went cabaret hopping with an infallible sense of indirection. I think we hit every back-street dive in Paris. Parisian taxi drivers have questionable taste in nightclubs; they kept taking us to strange-looking places and assuring us they were "magnifique." Most of them had blue lights; most of them were smoke-filled and had at least two or three patrons who were slumped forward, dozing face down at their tables; most of them had nude variety acts on small stages, which was incredible for the fifties; and all of them had a full complement of prostitutes who were magnetically attracted to Bogie, whether they recognized him or not.

It was weird. I don't know what there was about Bogie that prostitutes found so attractive, but as soon as we entered a joint, they all made a beeline for him, abruptly leaving their disgruntled admirers, which didn't sit well with them and caused a couple of near-fights. Bogie was fascinated with the Parisian prostitutes and always found someone who could speak English so that he could interview them, asking how and why they had chosen their line of work. Each told him her life story in great detail, and there were some very funny and some heartrending stories. It was a strange night but not a boring one; Bogie got more propositions than a Hollywood starlet at a producers' stag party. He declined their offers gallantly, telling each of them that while he was overpowered by their allure, I, whom he introduced as his mistress, would have his scalp if he fell victim to their obvious and almost irresistible charm. Then he'd lift the back of his toupee to show them that he wasn't exaggerating.

At four A.M. we finally headed for Les Halles, the old market district of Paris. We found a small corner café, where we ate onion soup and sobered up a bit and watched the hustle and bustle of the marketplace, which came alive while most Parisians were sleeping. Then we went back to the Ritz and had a nightcap— which we hardly needed—before going to bed.

It was nearly noon when I was awakened by the phone. It was the airline, informing us that we could get a flight to Rome earlier than anticipated. I had to postpone Bogie's meeting with General Gunther until our return to Paris after the picture was finished. We bathed and packed and had our luggage sent to the airport. I was autographing photos of Bogie to leave at the desk for people to pick up when a cable from Betty arrived. She said she hoped he was having fun and that she couldn't wait to join him in Italy.

"Wire her back for me," Bogie said. "Say something sweet and charming, in my usual style and manner."

"I'll tell her how you're such a hit with prostitutes," I said.

I grabbed a cable blank and wrote: "Miss you, love you, miss you, love you; hurry over. (signed) Bogie." I called the concierge and had the cable sent off; then we went to the Berkeley for breakfast. We ordered Bloody Marys and eggs Benedict. Bogie was a little down and quiet, more from lack of sleep than from drink. We had another Bloody Mary and, as usual, ate less than half our food. "Hell, Pete," Bogie said. "You and I ought to always order children's portions; we eat like birds."

Then we flew off to Rome.

13

Italy

The weather turned bad again, and we had a four-hour delay at Orly before we were finally airborne. We were still exhausted from our night on the town, so we both slept on the plane. I awoke before Bogie and filled out the necessary customs and immigration papers. I woke him when we began circling Rome's Ciampino Airport. He stretched and looked out the window; it was night now and raining like hell. "I doubt that we'll be bothered by newsmen tonight," he said.

We were among the last to leave the plane and had to dash through the downpour to the immigration and medical cubicles, where we were kept waiting. We were met by a man named George Seabury when we finally reached customs. Seabury spoke Italian, and his stature alone was intimidating enough to get us through customs faster than usual—he was six-foot-seven. He was with Figaro, the company that was producing *The Barefoot Contessa*. "There's a Mr. Herd waiting for you with a car and driver," Seabury told us.

We met Jim Herd in the airport lobby; he was the publicity man for *Barefoot*. "I'm sorry there's no press here tonight," he told Bogie.

Bogie looked around the lobby. "Gee," he said, "that's too bad. I thought I'd be mobbed by the press."

"It's late," Herd said apologetically, "and the weather's really bad, you know."

"Knock off the phony excuses, ol' boy," Bogie said. "If I were Ava Gardner, those news bastards would *swim* out here if that's what it took. What'd you say your line is? *Publicity?*"

I suspect that Jim Herd had been told about Bogie by someone, for he surprised us both with his response. "That's right, Mr. Bogart," he said. "Publicity. But this is an international production, so the union calls for Italian personnel, too. I'm fair-weather publicity; they've got an Italian doing foul-weather publicity, but he couldn't make it tonight because of the foul weather."

Bogie laughed. "Well, I'll be damned!" he said. "A publicity creep with a sense of humor. Never thought I'd see the day. Okay, Mr. Herd, you've got my number. I really don't give a big rat's ass about the newsmen, but I *was* sort of looking forward to meeting the Mafia. Any of the Mafia here to greet me?"

Herd laughed. "I don't have much influence with the Mafia," he said. "Anyway, they probably skipped town when they heard that the tough guy was coming to Rome."

"Yeah. You're probably right. I am an intimidating son of a bitch. They probably got on a fleet of planes bound for Chicago. I hope they didn't take the city's supply of Scotch with 'em. Have you met Pete here?"

We shook hands. "Nice to meet you, Pete," Herd said.

"She's my executive secretary, adviser, and mistress. I threw in that last to give you something to write about. I know how you publicity creeps like dirt."

We thanked Seabury and invited him to join us at the hotel for a nightcap, but he had other things to do at the airport and said he'd take a raincheck. Herd drove us to the Excelsior Hotel and dropped us off. The porters took our luggage to our suites, and Bogie followed them as I sent a cable off to Betty, telling her we had arrived safely. When I got up to our floor, I heard Bogie's voice booming down the hallway from the open door to his suite. He was talking to the porter, who spoke no English, and I guess Bogie felt that if he talked louder, he'd somehow get through to the poor guy.

When I entered, the porter was rattling off something in Italian, and Bogie was perplexed.

"What's the matter?" I said.

"Twin beds!" Bogie said, motioning toward them. "Talk to the bastard, will you, Pete? Tell him I want a big double bed in here."

"Are you kidding? I don't speak Italian."

"Speak to him in Mexican, then—something. But tell him I want a big bed."

The porter was more frustrated than Bogie; he obviously wanted to please him. I tried to explain Bogie's wishes, using Spanish, and after a moment the porter's face lit up with a big smile. "Ah. *Sì, sì, signorina,*" he said, and rushed out of the suite.

"Is he going to get it or what?" Bogie said.

"Hell, I don't know."

Moments later the porter returned with a helper. They rushed around, removed the nightstand from between the beds, then pushed the beds tightly together. This was accompanied by great smiles and triumphant bows to me.

"Christ!" Bogie said. "Now look what you've done."

"Me? You're lucky they didn't both come back and crap in your hat! How do I know what they think I'm saying? At least they're getting close to understanding."

I began with the Spanish again and threw in a little pantomime. Finally the porter got the picture. "Ah. *Sì! A domani, signorina,*" he said.

"He says 'tomorrow,' " I translated.

Bogie gave up in disgust. "I wish they'd learn to speak English," he said.

"We're the foreigners," I said. "I'll get an extra blanket and bridge the gap between the beds; it'll do until tomorrow."

The twin beds turned out to be not only an inconvenience but also an embarrassment. We had a continental breakfast sent up the following morning and had just finished eating when Bogie began teasing me about something. We got into a wrestling match, and I was getting the better of him. He was weak from laughter, rolled over, the beds parted, and he sank out of sight between them. I was still after him, and he was just crawling out backward from between the beds when the door suddenly opened and one of the hotel maids stepped in and froze in her tracks. Bogie was on his hands and knees, backing out from between the beds, his bare ass pointed directly at the maid. I guess I gasped. He craned his neck around, spotted her, and dove between the beds again. The red-faced maid jumped back into the sitting room and slammed the door without a word. It was hysterical, and I was doubled up with laughter. Bogie was lying facedown between the beds when I finally regained composure; I crawled to the edge of the bed and looked down at him. "You okay?" I said.

His voice, muffled by the blanket that he had his face buried in, drifted up to me. "Oh, sure," he said, "just swell."

I was overcome with laughter again but managed to assure him that he had nothing to worry about. "She had a rear view and probably didn't recognize you," I said. "She probably mistook your ass for your face—I know I often do."

Bogie began laughing and climbed up after me; the wrestling match was on again. I teased him about the incident for a week. We were walking toward the elevator a couple of days later and spotted a cleaning cart in the hall; the maid was in a suite, cleaning, but the door was open. As we hurried past the door, I said to Bogie, "Don't drop your pants or she'll recognize you."

Later in the morning of the twin-bed incident, Johnny Johnson, production manager for *The Barefoot Contessa,* came up to the suite. I had worked with Johnny on a picture or two before, but Bogie hadn't. I told Bogie that Johnny was one of the best production managers in the business and a very nice guy. Surprisingly, after I'd introduced them, Bogie didn't needle Johnny at all.

Johnny told Bogie that he wouldn't be on call until the next day and that he might as well take the opportunity to do a little sightseeing.

"Did you bring the dough?" Bogie asked him.

"Yes," Johnny said. He pulled out a wad of lire that would have choked a hippopotamus and gave it to Bogie, who in turn handed it to me to count. Bogie's contract for the picture called for all reasonable expenses to be paid by the production company, plus the equivalent of a thousand American dollars a week pocket money. Since a lira was equivalent to only eight or nine American cents in those days, it took me the length of Johnny's visit to count the damn stuff. Meanwhile, Johnny kidded Bogie about finding enough time to spend that much money each week, since he'd be busy making a film.

"Hell," Bogie said, "I couldn't do it, but Baby will be here in a couple of weeks, and she'll go through this stuff faster than the government can print it—unless she gets exhausted lugging it around and counting it."

Before he left, Johnny said that Bogie and I had been invited to dinner, a big affair that the picture's director, Joseph L. Mankiewicz (who also wrote the screenplay), was giving at his villa that night. Then Johnny gave me the shooting schedule and said to Bogie, "There's a car and driver at the hotel entrance; they're at your disposal for the duration of the picture. The driver's name is Nino, and he speaks English."

"Thank God for that," Bogie said, eyeing the twin beds that would be replaced that afternoon.

After Johnny left, Bogie suggested that we dismiss Nino and the car until it was time for the Mankiewicz dinner. "Let's stroll the Via Veneto and see if we can get into a little trouble; then we can go to George's for lunch," he said.

George's was a restaurant near the Excelsior that

specialized in American dishes. There was an American bar there and a bartender who spoke English. The food was excellent, and a charming elderly Italian gentleman played the guitar until the place closed in the wee hours of the morning. Like Romanoff's or 21, George's became Bogie's headquarters, and with few exceptions, we ate dinner there every night while we were in Rome.

The Mankiewicz dinner that evening was lovely. We met the producer of *Barefoot,* Robert Haggiag, and a number of Italian and American celebrities. Angelo Rizzoli, the editor of the Italian magazine *Europa* (who was also one of the picture's principal backers), told Bogie that he wanted to do an article and picture layout of him in the magazine. "Okay," Bogie said, "but none of that cheesecake stuff or debauched stuff. I've seen how some of these Italian publications treat American actors and actresses—their pictures are always taken through the bottom of shot glasses or when they're smoking marijuana or something." Rizzoli assured Bogie that he'd be treated with dignity.

Bogie made the rounds at the party, good-naturedly needling everybody, including the director and the producer, but he spent much of the evening with a priest named Father McCarthy, who was an aide to the Vatican. Happily, the padre had an excellent sense of humor, for Bogie's approach to him was typically Bogart. He noticed the padre sitting alone, dropped into a chair next to him, clinked his glass against the padre's as though in toast, and said, "Here's looking up your old address, Father."

Father McCarthy was fascinated with the making of motion pictures and asked Bogie countless questions about the process. Before the evening was through, Bogie was trying to convince him that while acting was a noble profession, the picture business was phony, as were most of the people in it. As proof, Bogie pointed to his own head. "Even this hair is phony," he said. "Pete, here, puts it on." Father McCarthy marveled at how real it looked, and Bogie explained to him how it was applied. "The damn thing really stays on, too," Bogie told him. "Of course, it has to. Can you imagine my making love and the muff falling down over my eyes so that I couldn't see what I was doing?"

I tried to sink into my chair as the padre contemplated what Bogie had said. Finally he gave Bogie a charming smile and said, "I believe I'd prefer imagining something on a bit higher philosophical plane."

"Oh, yeah," Bogie said. "Well, of course, I was referring to love scenes in *motion pictures.*"

"Of course," Father McCarthy said, smiling.

All during the evening, Bogie kept turning to me and saying loud enough for the padre to hear, "Watch this guy, Pete. He's smart and might try to convert us." And at one point, he looked at the padre's robe and said, "What the hell do you wear under there, pants?"

The father smiled. "Yes," he said. "Doesn't everyone?"

Bogie had an early-morning call, so, for a change, we were among the first to leave the party. On the way back to the hotel, Bogie said, "That Father McCarthy's a good Joe, isn't he?"

"Yes," I said, "but you could have been a little more diplomatic with him."

"Oh, hell, Pete. Everybody tiptoes around someone like that. Must be boring as hell for him. How would you like being treated like some goddamned saint or some-thing? People bowing and scraping and not being themselves at all around you? I think he enjoyed talking to me; I know I did with him. Probably the first un-guarded conversation he's had since he hooked up with the Vatican."

"Yeah. Particularly that part about your muff not fall-ing off when you're making love."

Bogie chuckled. "Yeah, well, I really *did* mean dur-ing love scenes on the set. Kind of shook him up there for a minute, though, didn't I?"

"Let's just say that the good padre won't forget the conversation," I said.

Nino, the driver, was waiting for us early the next morning. Bogie had complained the night before about the little Alpha Romeo the studio had furnished, but we had assumed that it was the only car available for the dinner party. "Christ!" Bogie said as we came out of the hotel, "they've given us that damn toy car again. There's barely enough room in it for my feet and ass, let alone my balls!"

The car's size wasn't our only problem. Nino drove like a Grand Prix racer. Ordinarily the drive from the hotel to Cinecitta Studios would take about forty-five minutes. Nino made it in about twenty. He took off like a bat out of hell, skidding around corners, swerving around pedestrians, ignoring traffic signals and other motorists, foot to the floorboard and hand on the horn. He scared hell out of us. He was apparently of the philosophy that using brakes wasn't macho. We proba-bly went as fast as seventy miles an hour in the city, but

I'm not positive; my eyes were riveted on the road ahead.

When we finally skidded to a stop at the studio, Bogie and I broke records getting out of the damn car. We had screamed at Nino several times to slow down. But slow to him was about fifty—in the city; he seemed a little disappointed that getting us to the studio at record speed wasn't greatly appreciated. He was a good-natured kid with a big disarming grin, and he nodded and grinned and grinned and nodded as Bogie was chewing him out. "This goddamned car is no bigger than a casket on wheels," he told Nino. "One accident at the speed you drive, and they'll just dig a hole and drop us into it, car and all. You seem like a nice kid, but frankly I don't want to be buried with you."

When Bogie finished his lecture, he slammed the car door, and Nino took off like a bat out of hell again. Bogie watched the car screech around the corner. "Something tells me I didn't get through to him," he said.

Nobody greeted us upon our arrival at the studio, so we wandered around until we found its dressing-room row. The doors were closed but lettered with the names of the *Barefoot* cast: Ava Gardner, Edmond O'Brien, Rossano Brazzi, Warren Stevens, Mari Aldon (director Tay Garnett's wife), and others. Bogie's room wasn't much by Hollywood standards—just one room with a dressing table, a bed, a bathroom, and a closet. I made a mental note to have a few things brought in, including a refrigerator for Bogie's beer, then went to work applying his toupee.

When the makeup man finished with him, we went over to Ava Gardner's dressing room to say hello. Ava had brought along a sizable entourage, including bullfighter Luís Miguel. She was a lovely woman, and friendly, but quiet and reserved. I liked her, and so did Bogie. We didn't see much of her off the set, though, except glimpses of her leaving or entering the hotel with her entourage, or tribe, as Bogie called them.

Ava greeted Bogie warmly. "My, you look fit and as trim as Sinatra," she said.

"Nobody's as trim as Sinatra," Bogie said. "And how come he's not here?" Bogie added. "I'll never figure you broads out. Half the world's female population would throw themselves at Frank's feet, and here you are flouncing around with guys who wear capes and little ballerina slippers."

"Aren't you being just a bit nosy?" Ava said, arching an eyebrow.

"Sure. But what the hell else is there to talk about in Italy?"

As she would throughout the making of the picture, Ava took Bogie's needling coolly and good-naturedly. Not once did he get the best of her. But he tried. It was getting close to call time, and Ava's "tribe" was beginning to cluster around, so Bogie said, "Let me get a running start toward the set. I don't want to get trampled by your entourage. And if I waited until it passed, I wouldn't get to the set until Thursday."

"I'll give you a ten-second head start," Ava said. "Then you're on your own."

The carpenters and other craftsmen were buzzing around the set like flies when we arrived. Bogie stopped to talk to cinematographer Jack Cardiff. "Do you favor any particular side?" Cardiff asked Bogie.

"Nah. One side of me is as ugly as the other, ol' boy," Bogie said. "Just try to get my mug in the scene once in a while, and not too many crotch shots, okay?"

Cardiff laughed. "That's a tall order," he said.

Bogie groaned at the pun. "You might keep an eye out for shiny spots on this hair lace, though. Pete will keep it covered, but she can't see all the angles. And don't light up to eliminate the lines from my face, okay? Took me a long time to get them, and I'm not the fucking Casanova in this picture, you know."

"Damn!" Cardiff said. "I better read the script again. I missed the part about fucking Casanova."

Bogie laughed. "I'll be damned," he said. "A cameraman with a sense of humor. We may have some fun on this job after all."

We went over to the portable dressing room and peeked in. It was a tentlike affair, with nothing inside but a cot, a dressing table, and a dirt floor. Bogie looked at it and said, "What the hell is *this,* an Italian toilet?"

While the crew was getting ready to shoot, we made the portable dressing room as comfortable as possible. We got a bucket of ice and an ice pick, a heater—for it was cold and damp—some bottled Italian water, and the like. We drank the bottled water only the first day; it gave us the Roman trots, and we settled for bottled club soda after that.

Ava was very popular with the Italian crew and made a sensational entrance. Behind her, of course, was her entourage, which consisted of her sister Beatrice, the bullfighter Luís Miguel, a wardrobe person, a couple of makeup people—as though she really needed them—and a few others, laden with stacks of flamenco and Sinatra records and Ava's record player.

The first scene shot was on a set representing a cheap Casablanca cabaret, where Ava, portraying a flamenco dancer, is discovered by Bogie, portraying a recovered-alcoholic movie director. I needled Bogie about laying off the loudmouth so he could psych himself up for the role, and he told me what I could do with the suggestion and with anything else large and square within reach. "It's times like this that I thank God I'm not one of those new breed—the method actors who have to live the part," he said. Someone once asked Bogie if he had ever tried to stop drinking, and he said, "Yes. And it was the worst afternoon of my life."

Ava Gardner was summoned to the set by the assistant director, Pierre Menzetto, and she stepped from her dressing room wearing a bright blue and red gypsy-style dress and Spanish earrings. She was barefoot and wore her hair long and brushed straight. She went into her flamenco routine and riveted the attention of everyone on the set—which isn't easy to do with blasé professionals; about the only other actress I've seen accomplish that is Elizabeth Taylor. Both women are as stunning off screen as on. It was obvious that Ava had put a great deal of time and effort into the choreography, but I doubt that the males present paid much attention to her footwork.

Bogie was impressed with her preparation, too, but that didn't stop him from needling her. Between takes, he addressed her as the Crabtown gypsy (Ava was born in a small Southern town) and told her that the reason she didn't drink much with us was because her Southern accent slipped out when she drank and she was afraid that her bullfighters would discover that she was just a "li'l hillbilly girl."

"That's what attracts 'em, honey chil'," Ava said.

That first day's shooting was spent doing the cabaret

scene over and over, as usual. At the end of the day, we crammed back into the Alpha Romeo with Nino for a hair-raising ride back to the Excelsior. This time, though, we at least kept Nino from breaking the sound barrier by nagging constantly at him.

We were checking with the hotel desk for messages when an old friend, actor Bruce Cabot, hailed Bogie. Cabot had been an army lieutenant in North Africa when Bogie and Mayo made a brief USO trip there during the war; he was now living in Italy. Cabot was introducing his girl friend to us when someone sneaked up behind us and tapped us both on the shoulder. We turned to find Errol Flynn. "I'll be damned!" Bogie said, laughing and shaking hands with Flynn. "These Italians will let *any* son of a bitch into their country, won't they!"

Flynn winked and kissed me on the cheek. "Getting *into* Italy is easy," he said. "It's getting out that's tough."

"Well, c'mon, you son of a bitch," Bogie said. "Let's have a drink, and you can bring me up to date on your latest adventures."

We went into the Excelsior's downstairs bar. Flynn ordered martinis; Bogie, Cabot, his girl, and I ordered loudmouth. We learned that Killer and Cabot had formed a partnership and were producing a film about William Tell. "The bloody thing's in neutral at the moment," Flynn said. "We went into business with a bunch of fucking Italians. Got a quarter of the way through the picture, and they claimed to have run out of money. They were trying to milk us for more, which we don't have. I'd sunk all my cash into the damn thing and pushed my credit to the limit. Then I had no sooner dumped the crooked bastards when Uncle Sam jumped on me again, and my ex-wife started giving me trouble on the alimony racket again. So I can't go back to the States at the moment. At least here I can stay one jump ahead of the creditors and eat."

Flynn finished his drink. "I've got to see a man about some financing," he said, pulling lire from his pocket to pay the check.

"Your money's no good here," Bogie said. "I'm working. This goes on my tab. But listen, why don't you guys get your unsavory business out of the way and meet us over at George's for dinner?"

"May we bring our broads?" Flynn asked.

"I wouldn't recognize you *without* a broad. Better yet, come back here to the hotel at seven and have a smash, then we'll all walk over to George's together."

"Great," Flynn said. "We'll do that. Thanks for the drink, and I'll see you guys later. Keep your peckers up."

Bogie decided to make it a big dinner party, and so he invited Rossano Brazzi, the Mankiewiczs, Mari Aldon (Tay was busy in London), and the Eddie O'Briens. We had a fine time, and the evening was marred only by Bogie's needling of Mari Aldon—mostly about her marrying an "old man" like Tay Garnett. It was absurd, considering that Mari and Tay were no further apart in years than Bogie and Betty. But Mari was sweet and thin-skinned, and Bogie's needle penetrated deeper than he had intended. She left the table in tears, and I bugged Bogie into apologizing to her. "All right, all right," Bogie said, going after her. "You broads are all alike. No sense of humor." Bogie's apology didn't work; Mari fled to her room.

Italy

Flynn surprised me at dinner by asking Bogie how John Huston was getting along. Flynn and Huston had had a notorious marathon fistfight at a Hollywood party one time, and I had wrongly assumed that there was bad blood between them. From the tenor of the dinner-table conversation about Huston, it was clear that Flynn had gained a good deal of respect for him—Huston had once been a professional fighter—and that he liked Huston almost as much as Bogie did.

We left the dinner party early and walked back to the Excelsior. On the way, I got pinched on the ass. By reflex, I stepped back, swung my purse, and hit Bogie on the side of the head. It hit him with a resounding thump.

"Jesus, Pete!" Bogie yelled. "You gone nuts or something?"

"Hell, no," I said. "You know how goosy I am. What'd you pinch me for?"

Bogie felt the side of his head and examined his hand to see if I'd drawn blood; I hadn't. Then he started to laugh. "I didn't pinch you, you silly broad."

"Then who did?"

He looked up the street. A couple of men had passed us. "You've got an Italian admirer," he said. "Ass pinching is a custom here, didn't you know that?"

I had known of the "quaint" custom but hadn't thought about it. Bogie was still feeling his face, and I felt terrible. I had really thumped him a good one. "I'm sorry, sweetheart," I said. "I did it by reflex."

"Yeah, I'll bet," he said. "Damn! You don't even know your own strength!"

When we got back to the hotel, I noticed he had a

raised bruise above his cheekbone, so I ordered ice sent up and applied it to keep the swelling down. Eddie O'Brien and his wife stopped in for a nightcap, and Bogie entertained them with stories about how I carried bricks in my purse and attacked innocent people without provocation.

Later that night, I began worrying about Bogie's having to go before the camera the following morning. A couple of times I turned on the bedside lamp to check the swelling; I had visions of it ballooning to the size of a melon. But it didn't swell. I thought I had checked without disturbing him, but the second time I turned the light on, he rolled over, squinted open one eye, and fixed it on me. "What the hell is this, Pete? Some kind of Nazi torture or something? First you beat the hell out of me, then you shine a light in my eyes all night! I gotta work in the morning, remember?"

I apologized, turned the lamp off, and rolled over, content that the swelling was under control. Then Bogie mumbled something.

"What?" I said.

"Your purse. Where is it?"

"My purse? It's on the dresser. Why?"

"Just wanted to be sure it's out of reach," he said. Then he pinched me on the ass.

Bogie's morning call at the studio was canceled, so we decided to sightsee. While Bogie was in the shower, I put in a call to Father McCarthy to see if he could arrange an audience with the Pope, which is something everyone tries to do in Rome. We were having breakfast in the suite when the padre called back; we had an appointment at the Vatican in one hour. I told Bogie what I'd done.

"My God, Pete, I don't want to be responsible for the Vatican roof caving in," he said.

"C'mon," I said. "Like Killer says, 'God hates a coward.'"

"Yeah. That's exactly what worries me."

I hurriedly applied his toupee, then started for my suite to change. I hadn't dressed for an audience with the Pope.

"Hey," Bogie said. "What am I supposed to wear to this shindig?"

"Oh, I forgot," I said. "Father McCarthy says for me to wear a dress and veil and for you to wear a conservative suit and tie."

I dashed to my suite, dressed, messed with my hair, gave up on it in despair, and returned to Bogie's suite. He was ready to go. "How do I look?" he said.

"The suit's fine, but that tie's gotta go."

He picked up the end of his tie and looked at it. "What the hell's wrong with this tie?" he said. "I like it."

"It looks like something you won by breaking balloons with darts at a carnival," I said.

I searched for a more conservative tie. A bow tie didn't seem appropriate, and he hadn't brought that many regular ties with him. "See if I've got one in there with little red devils on it," he said.

"It wouldn't surprise me." I finally found one that I thought would do, and as he was changing it, he said, "Do we have to kneel and kiss the papal ring?"

"No. Only Catholics do that."

"Maybe I'll just curtsy, then."

"You do, Bogie, and I'll hit you with my purse on purpose."

Nino got us to the Vatican in his usual record time, and Bogie spent a couple of minutes cussing him out. Nino sat behind the wheel, nodding and flashing his beautifully white teeth. Cussing Nino out for speeding became a daily routine. Bogie could have had him replaced in a moment, but the damn kid had a wife and a couple of bambinos, I think, and a happy-go-lucky attitude that was ingratiating. Besides, I think Bogie secretly enjoyed the thrill of Nino's crazy driving. If John Huston had known about Nino, he would probably have hired him for life; like Bogie, Huston seemed to enjoy dangerous challenges. Actually, to be fair, Nino was a skillful driver; he knew exactly what he was doing, but the problem was that his passengers didn't know that he knew. He would have been a great New York cabby, and he'd probably have made a fortune at it. Even so, a short drive with Nino at the wheel pumped enough adrenaline into the bloodstream to last a month.

We bought a few medals for the Pope to bless for friends back in the States and were received along with a large number of people. Our audience lasted only a minute or so. I'm happy to report that Bogie did not pull a rib on Pope Pius XII.

A few days later, Bogie invited Gina Lollobrigida to lunch at the studio commissary. Gina had been in *Beat the Devil* with Bogie. She was a lovely, talented, and sensuous woman (owing to the size of her breasts, Bogie nicknamed her "Low Bridge," and Gina, who had trouble pronouncing Bogie, called him "Boogie"), and she had a delicious sense of humor. They discussed the filming of *Beat the Devil* all through lunch, and I could hardly eat for laughing.

I had been to Italy with them at the beginning and had done Bogie's hairpieces for the film, but the filming was delayed and I didn't stay; I think I had committed to another picture. Anyway, in Bogie's view, the shooting was a disaster, but the film itself is now considered a classic—an underground classic, anyway—and rightly so, I think. In its day, though, it was neither critically nor financially successful. I've read that some people have claimed that Bogie hated the picture and is alleged to have said that anyone who liked it was stupid, or words to that effect. This just isn't true. Bogie may have made such a statement as a joke, and certainly he hated the making of it, but he liked the finished product. With a director like John Huston (who also did some work on the screenplay), a writer like Truman Capote, and stars like Gina Lollobrigida, Peter Lorre, Robert Morley, and Jennifer Jones, the film's box-office failure (at the time) was bewildering, and Bogie was disappointed. But as John Huston recently noted in his autobiography, *An Open Book,* the satire of the film was lost on the fifties movie audience. Huston feels that the film was probably twenty years ahead of its time, and its current popularity bears him out.

Both Gina and Bogie loved telling tales of working with Truman Capote. Bogie had been indifferent to Capote at first, but by the end of the picture, Bogie considered Capote one of his closest friends. "Truman's a guy I'd like to have around all the time," Bogie once told me. "There's never a dull moment with him around, and he'd be handy if a fight broke out, too; he's a tough little bastard, and he's got enough guts for three guys twice his size."

During the filming of *Devil,* Capote apparently had

to leave his talking bird in Rome. I don't know whether it was a parrot or a myna, but Capote loved it and often called his housekeeper to have her put the bird on the phone. One day the bird refused to talk to him; Capote didn't know whether the bird was sick or just in a snit, but he was so worried that he stopped writing the script during production of the film and took off for Rome to see for himself.

"I thought it was a ploy to stall the picture," Bogie said at the luncheon with Gina, "but I hear the bird died, so I guess it was for real. I never knew what Double Ugly (his affectionate nickname for Huston) and Truman were up to for sure."

Truman's bird may well have been sick, but Bogie's suspicions were well founded regarding Huston's efforts to stall the filming. When we first got to Italy, Huston leveled with Bogie; he told him that he didn't have a suitable script for the picture, but Bogie wanted to wing it. Santana Productions had purchased the film rights to James Helvick's novel, but it proved difficult to adapt. Huston, dissatisfied with other screenwriters' attempts, finally decided to work on it himself, and he enlisted Capote's aid. Even so, the writing went slowly, and Huston admits devising various ploys to stall the production during the filming rather than risk demoralizing the actors by telling them that there were no words on paper for them to film.

The biggest fiasco, though, was the auto accident in which Bogie was injured; that alone gave him nightmares about filming *Beat the Devil.* The cast was moving from one location in Italy to another. Bogie and Huston traveled together in one car, chauffeured by an Italian driver who presumably knew the roads. They had been en route for a while when Bogie decided to nap in the back seat. While he was sleeping, the chauffeur came to a fork in the road and, unsure of which branch to take, he apparently decided on one direction, changed his mind, and lost control of the car, which went straight ahead through a stone wall.

Bogie was thrown against the back of the front seats, knocking out his upper bridge, which contained two teeth, and cutting a terrible U-shaped gash in the top of his tongue, a gash that Huston said flapped like a little trap door and that had to be stitched up at a nearby hospital. The picture was delayed for a week until a new dental bridge arrived from Bogie's dentist in California.

Huston tells of the accident in his autobiography. He says that when the dust settled after they went through the stone wall (neither Huston nor the chauffeur was hurt), and after he had determined that Bogie wasn't critically injured, the absurdity of the accident struck him and he began laughing. Bogie looked at him, and through the gap where his two front teeth had been, he said, "John, you thun of a bith! You dirty thun of a bith!"

To hear Bogie relate the incident again to Gina was hilarious. It had been less than a year since the accident, and Bogie showed Gina his two new front teeth. "What do you think of them? Good job, huh?" Bogie said.

"You don't look a damn bit better to me, Boogie," she said.

Bogie also told Gina about our regular driver, Nino. "If I didn't know better," he said, "I'd swear that Huston hired that son of a bitch for me."

It was only a day or two later that Bogie got a message that John Huston and Peter Lorre were in Rome, apparently just passing through. Bogie called them and invited them to dinner at George's. I never got to know John Huston well, and I'm sorry for that, but judging from the way Bogie liked him and talked about him, he's a wonderfully fascinating man. The couple of times that I did meet him, he was very quiet, almost introspective. But then with Bogie and Lorre needling one another, anyone would seem quiet—it was hard to get a word in edgewise with those two around. Unfortunately, about the only thing I recall from the dinner at George's that evening is that there was a very elegantly dressed and bejeweled woman in the place who caught everyone's attention. Bogie surmised that she was a countess or some such. The irrepressible Lorre disagreed. "I'll bet she's a hooker," he said. They argued for a few minutes and then finally made a ten-dollar bet. To settle the argument, both of them had nerve enough to approach the woman and ask her. She recognized them and was flattered at the attention. Lorre won the bet.

We were into the filming about three weeks or so when Betty arrived. She got off the plane carrying a large coconut cake for Ava Gardner, a present from Sinatra for her birthday. Betty got a little miffed about that cake. She had felt responsible for her charge and had hand-carried it by taxi and limousine and several thousand miles across the Atlantic by plane to ensure its arrival in one piece. And when she finally presented it to Ava, Ava thanked her but pushed it aside and didn't even open the box. The action was so uncharacteristic of Ava that we figured it signaled the end of her relationship with Frank.

Naturally, my social life changed complexion when

Betty arrived. I went out shopping with her a couple of times, and the three of us went sightseeing or to dinner or for drinks occasionally, but for the most part, I began going out with friends who were working on *Barefoot* and with friends of mine or Walter's who happened to be vacationing in Rome.

Betty drove Bogie to distraction with her shopping. A typical husband, he bitched and moaned every time she returned to the hotel with packages. As anyone would, Betty was taking advantage of the then-low European prices for goods that would have cost a fortune back in the States. But Bogie, whose manager had him on a strict budget and who was always strapped for cash, hated to see his expense money going for "unimportant" things like clothing and jewelry. "Look, Baby," he kept saying, "don't be spending all the money."

"But things are so cheap here."

"Oh, sure," Bogie said. "Why not get a dozen of everything so we can open a goddamned clothing store when we get back."

Bogie was particularly upset when Betty bought clothes for the children. "Swell," he'd say. "I'm glad you got enough stuff so that they'll be grown out of it before they have to wear everything more than once."

Betty loved to shop, and there was no pleasing Bogie on that score. She returned one day and told him that she had bought him some Italian silk shirts—a dozen each of white, blue, and purple. "Christ!" he said. "You'll have me looking like an Italian pimp!"

Considering Bogie's penchant for needling people, it's surprising that he didn't get into any trouble in

Rome; he probably would have had he spoken Italian. It was I, not Bogie, who managed to become persona non grata at the Excelsior's downstairs bar. Bogie was very smug about that, telling me that I was bringing dishonor by association to a "star"; I retaliated by reminding him that in his earlier drinking days, he had been barred from *Hollywood Reporter* owner Billy Wilkerson's clubs and had once been briefly barred from 21. So I wasn't setting any precedent by getting bounced from the Excelsior bar. And as Bogie admitted, it was a bum rap.

I had gone to dinner with actor Dennis O'Keefe and his wife, both of whom I knew and who were on vacation. Afterward we made the rounds of the nightclubs, then returned to the Excelsior for a nightcap. There were only two other customers in the place—a couple of American men drinking at the bar. The O'Keefes and I were minding our own business, having a drink and telling smutty stories. We were in a festive mood and laughing a lot when one of the Americans said loudly, "I hate dirty cornball actors who don't have to do a damn thing but get their pictures taken and sit around drinking and telling dirty stories."

Dennis raised his voice without so much as casting a glance toward the guys at the bar. "And I hate creeps who get overly courageous and big-mouthed when they've put a couple of Shirley Temples under their belts."

The reply was a drink thrown at Dennis. The men were at the end of the bar, a distance away, so the drink fell short and the glass shattered on the floor. Dennis jumped up and started after the guys. One of them ran out the door while the other—the big mouth—reached behind the bar and pulled out a bottle, threatening to cut Dennis's head off if he took another step.

Dennis didn't even hesitate. He grabbed a chair and circled the guy with the bottle. Mrs. O'Keefe began crying. I picked up a chair, too, figuring to outflank the guy and let him have it while he was circling Dennis. But fortunately, before I got there, Dennis took a swing with the chair and missed. The guy dropped the bottle and ran out of the bar; Dennis dropped the chair and ran after him. Mrs. O'Keefe and I were heading toward the door when Dennis returned, smiling. He had chased the guy out of the hotel. All of us, including the distraught bartender, converged on the door at once.

"Let's finish our nightcap," Dennis said.

"No," the bartender said. "I could have lost my license for an incident like this. You'll have to leave. I'm closing." He had the door keys in his hand.

"But we haven't finished our drinks," Dennis said. "Besides, it's not closing time."

"It is now," the bartender said. "I want you to leave, and none of you is welcome here again."

Dennis tried to reason with the man. We hadn't started the fight. The bartender was adamant and surly.

"But it was self-defense," Dennis said.

"You will leave now, or I'll call security."

Dennis shrugged and made a ladies-first motion to us, and as we filed out, he grabbed the keys, closed the door, and locked the bartender inside. The bartender was still hammering on the door when we left the hotel to have a nightcap elsewhere. Dennis was so mad that he threw the keys in the gutter as we walked along.

I told Bogie about the incident on the set the next day. He threatened to throw a big drinking party at the bar and to drag me along so that they could all sit around and drink and have fun watching me get tossed out on my ass. He didn't carry out the plot, though.

When we finished shooting at Cinecittà Studios, the cast split up for location shooting at San Remo and Portofino. Bogie wasn't needed at San Remo, so we went directly to Portofino, where we had a week off while they shot the San Remo location first.

Owing to Betty's presence and to the luggage we had to carry, the Alpha Romeo was replaced with a Cadillac. We drove to and from Portofino in comfort—and safety. Poor Nino was totally subdued by the enormity of the car, which didn't contribute to his fantasy of being a race-car driver. He drove so slowly that we no longer had to watch the road ahead in terror; we actually saw some of Italy for a change.

We stopped and rested in Portofino. We were there on my birthday in February, and the Bogarts gave me a party and a red suede jacket. I was touched. Only Bogie knew my birthday, and though he had a sentimental spot and cried at weddings, he wasn't one to fuss over or care much about these things. But he never forgot my birthday. One year he gave me a ring that I still have and cherish; it was like the ring that he inherited from his father and always wore. I had often admired the ring, and Bogie found one very much like it in an antique shop in San Pedro, and bought it for me.

The production company was finally driven from Portofino by rainy weather, and the wrap-up scenes for the picture were finished back at the studio in Rome. Then we flew back to Paris, where Bogie toured the nearby American base and where we took a brief vacation before flying back to Los Angeles. We hated to leave Paris in the spring, but we all had other pressing commitments.

Part Three

14

Prelude

In early 1955, after a few weeks' rest, Bogie signed to do *We're No Angels* at Paramount, with Joan Bennett and Peter Ustinov, and we went back to work.

Ustinov was fun to work with, and Bogie liked him very much; for some reason he reminded Bogie of Zero Mostel, with whom Bogie had done his final Warner Brothers picture, *The Enforcer.* Bogie always kidded Zero about his "courage," a pun Bogie came up with after telling Zero that it took a lot of guts for a man to have a belly like his. I guess Ustinov reminded Bogie of Zero because both men had an other-worldly zaniness about them; you never knew what they would do or say next. But unlike Zero, who was funny all the time and who was always on, Peter had his serious—and brilliant —side. He'd go along with ribs, but when Bogie put a piece of raw liver in his shoe one day, Peter wasn't exactly overjoyed. He didn't get mad at Bogie, but it was evident that he viewed that particular prank as juvenile (which it was).

"What's the matter, ol' boy?" Bogie said. "No sense of humor, huh?"

Zero might have done a ten-minute bit with the liver, but Peter just looked at him and said in mock dignity, "I rarely laugh at food."

Bogie also kidded Peter about being an Englishman. He'd affect what he thought to be an Oxford accent and give Peter a lecture on "bloody old England" and the questionable future of the British Empire. And Peter, who does a wonderful midwestern American accent, would make some wildly amusing retort that would have Bogie and me weak from laughter.

A few years after Bogie's death—and before Peter and my husband worked together—I ran into Peter and his wife, Suzanne, in Australia, where we had dinner together. I asked Peter if he remembered my association with Bogie, and he said, "Yes. You were his executive secretary." Peter was one of the few people in the industry who didn't know Bogie wore a toupee. We talked about Bogie's penchant for needling people, and Peter said, "You know, I think he did it from restlessness. Bogie always struck me as unhappy indoors, like a caged animal." I think that was a most telling assessment. Outdoors, and particularly at sea, Bogie was quite a different person. He still needled people, but not so often and never so earnestly.

We're No Angels was directed by Michael Curtiz, with whom Bogie had done four other motion pictures. Curtiz was a fine director and a fastidious man in his work and personal habits. He came to the United States from Europe and never mastered English; in fact, he mangled it. His and Samuel Goldwyn's malapropisms are legendary in Hollywood circles.

Prelude

Curtiz was constantly complaining about his portable dressing room. He was always after the cleaning crew, nagging them about the dirtiness of the floor. And he wouldn't even touch the couch that had been provided for him until it was cleaned. If he had had his way, there would have been a full-time cleaning person washing, mopping, vacuuming, and waxing his dressing room morning, noon, and night.

Bogie tired of hearing him complain about the alleged dirt, so he got a rubber or plastic dog turd somewhere, and while Curtiz was busy on the set, Bogie slipped into his dressing room and placed the fake dog turd on an overstuffed beige chair that Curtiz always used—his "dirty" couch had yet to be cleaned or replaced.

When Curtiz broke for lunch and went to his dressing room, Bogie, Ustinov, Aldo Ray, and I gathered near his door and waited for a reaction. It wasn't long in coming. The door suddenly burst open, and Curtiz propelled himself from it like a rocket, shouting, "Where is cleaning person? I want immediately the person who cleans!"

He started past Bogie, still yelling for the cleaning person, and Bogie grabbed his arm. "Hold on, Mike!" Bogie said. "What's going on here? You act like your pants are on fire or something."

"My God, Boogie," he said. (Like Gina Lollobrigida, he couldn't pronounce Bogie.) "I must find the person who cleans!"

"Cleans what?"

"My chair!" Curtiz said, trying to wrench from Bogie's grasp. "Boogie, a dog he has shit in my chair!"

Bogie guided him back into the dressing room.

"Where," he said. "How the hell can it be? We don't have any dogs on the set."

Curtiz pointed at his beige chair, where the fake dog turd nestled right in the center of the cushion. "There. See?" he said. "Some kind of small animal has did it if not a dog."

"Oh, yeah. I see. Well, hell, Mike, I'll take care of it for you."

Bogie walked over to the chair, picked up the fake turd, and slipped it into his pocket. I thought Curtiz was going to faint. Then Bogie rubbed his hands together and inspected them as though to see if any traces remained on his hands.

"There you go, Mike," he said. "What the hell are friends for if not to help in cases of emergency like this?"

Curtiz stared at Bogie with revulsion. And when Bogie lifted his hand to give him a friendly pat on the shoulder, Curtiz jerked back as though he didn't even want to associate with someone who would put dog turds in his pocket, let alone be touched by him.

Bogie had been gravely serious throughout, but when he started from the dressing room and spotted us —we were red-faced and writhing in pain, trying to keep from howling with laughter—he broke up. He pulled the fake turd from his pocket and, nearly doubled over with laughter, he pointed it at Curtiz. "By the way, Mike," he managed to say, "this is a prop."

Curtiz glared at him for a long moment, then shouted, "Boogie, you son of a beech!" And he slammed the door.

Our set was open for a while. That is, we had a lot of visitors, usually guests of studio personnel who wanted to see a Bogart film being made. Curtiz ended that arrangement one day while filming a particularly bothersome scene. It was a simple one. Joan Bennett was seated in a chair, and Bogie was to walk on, kneel down beside her, take her hand, and say, "Darling. . . ." and deliver the rest of the line. For some reason, the set didn't light to Curtiz and cinematographer Loyal Griggs's satisfaction, and after a number of false takes, Joe Connors, Bogie's stand-in, and Joan Bennett's stand-in were called to the set and went through the action over and over until the desired lighting was achieved.

Bennett took her place. The cameras rolled. Bogie came in, knelt, took Joan's hand and said, "Darling, the three of us have got to stop meeting like this." Joan Bennett stopped cold and stared at him, as did everyone else. The line wasn't in the script. Curtiz sputtered and cut the scene; the script girl just shrugged when Curtiz glared at her. There was general confusion until it was discovered that one of the women visitors was standing on her tiptoes and had inadvertently managed to get her head into the scene. Curtiz was so furious that he cleared the set of all visitors.

Occasionally Betty brought the children, Steve and Leslie, to the set. I always got a kick out of Bogie's reaction to them. They had appeared relatively late in his life—he was forty-nine when the first, Steve, was born, and fifty-two, I think, when Leslie came along. He looked upon them with a mixture of amusement and bewilderment. Like Gulliver, one day he awakened and found himself surrounded by little people, whom he couldn't quite figure out.

Bogie wasn't much for playing children's games and the like, though he tried. But his idea of playing with

Stevie was taking him to lunch at Romanoff's, which he often did. I'd give anything to have heard some of their conversations. In a way, Bogie's treatment of children was admirable; he addressed them like little people, and that's a hell of a lot better than the way I've seen many children treated by their parents.

One day Bogie said to me of Steve, "I don't think I'll ever understand that kid. Why in hell does he talk like that and tease his sister so?"

"You've got to be kidding!" I said. Stevie was going through a "little Bogie" phase, emulating his father. He was needling Leslie unmercifully and calling her creep and ol' girl—and a few other choice names that I'm sure earned him more than one mouthful of soap. I pointed out the irony of reaping what he had sown; he was being bugged by a midget version of himself. "God help us," I said, "when he comes of age. I don't think the world could take two Bogies."

"Hell, I'll never live to see them grown," he said.

He was right.

It was during the shooting of *We're No Angels* that I noticed a sore on the top of Bogie's ear. I mentioned it to him, and he said, "I figured you were scraping the top of my ear off with your comb." The next week it was still there and unchanged. "You ought to have this checked," I said. He said he had already made an appointment to do so. "It's probably skin cancer," he said. I tried to kid him out of it. I told him it was more than likely a venereal disease, but Bogie was right. It was a small skin cancer, which the doctor removed without complications.

It was about this same time that Bogie began having a dry cough and occasionally losing his voice—a hoarseness that bothered him a couple of times while he was making the picture. He attributed the symptoms to too many cigarettes, which seemed logical, since the cough did sound like a cigarette cough. But in fact they were the first symptoms of the disease that would take his life two years later.

I attended the Bogart Christmas party that year, and I'm glad I did. Bogie always said that such events were a way of killing two birds with one stone: celebrating Christmas and his birthday at the same time. By this time I had given up all hope of Bogie and me ever marrying. The birth of his second child, Leslie, two years earlier had put an end to my hope then. Looking back now, I can see that the birth of his first child was probably the determining factor, but that's hindsight; divorces where children are involved aren't uncommon, but given Bogie's moral code, it would have taken much more than whatever occasional disagreements he was having with Bacall for him to consider divorce. Bogie and I continued seeing each other because we wanted to, but after the birth of Stevie, the talk of divorce all but ended, and with Leslie's birth, it ended completely.

I arrived early for the Christmas party in order to apply Bogie's toupee. Betty was putting the finishing touches to the tree, and May was working her magic in the kitchen. Bogie hated caterers and preferred home-cooked meals for his get-togethers; they did add a particularly warm and homey touch that catered parties lacked.

It was a wonderful evening. Those of Bogie's close

friends who were in town were there. Sid Luft and Judy Garland, the Spencer Tracys, Frank Sinatra, Noel Coward, the David Nivens, Swifty Lazar, Peter Lorre, and others. We sang and drank and danced, with lots of conversation and lots of laughter. I had planned a white Christmas in New York and was leaving the following week, but during the party, I got a call from Walter. "I've arranged with the airline office to have a ticket waiting for you tomorrow for New York," he said.

"But I've already got my ticket—for next week."

"Never mind that," Walter said. "You haven't got any commitments out there for the rest of the week, have you?"

"Well, nothing important, but—"

"I've got a surprise for you that can't wait until next week. Please?"

I was thrilled and happy and agreed to leave for New York the next day. "But what's the surprise?" I said.

"Don't be nosy. Put Bogie on, will you?"

I called Bogie to the phone and stood by, hoping to learn something from his side of the conversation, but I could tell from the way he was talking that he was being cagy. When he finally hung up, I said, "What did he say?"

"He wished me and Betty a merry Christmas."

"You know what I mean. What's the surprise? Did he tell you?"

"Wouldn't you like to know."

I left the party early. I said good-bye to Betty and the others, and Bogie walked me out to my car. "That Walter's a hell of a good Joe, Pete," he said, opening the car door for me.

"I know he is."

"I mean, special," Bogie said. "And this Christmas surprise that he has for you—well, it's something you really need."

"What is it?"

"A new face," Bogie said.

"No, really."

"What kind of guy do you think I am, anyway? You know I wouldn't fink on Walter. Just remember what I said about it when you get it. It's something you really need."

"You know, Bogart, sometimes you can be a real pain in the ass."

Bogie leaned in and kissed me. "That's me, sweetheart," he said. "I've always been an ass man. Have a safe flight."

Walter was waiting with a limousine when my plane landed in New York. The chauffeur put my luggage in the trunk, and as we sped toward Manhattan, Walter handed me a small, foil-wrapped package. "Open it now," he said.

It was a magnificent diamond ring—an eight-and-a-half-carat marquis diamond. I started to take the ring from its case. "No, let me put it on you," he said.

In a daze, I held out my hand, and Walter shook his head. "I've got you cornered in a speeding sedan this time," he said. "No more diversionary tactics; wrong hand." He took my left hand and slipped the ring on my third finger. "This is an engagement ring, darling," he said. "The matching ring is in my pocket. I'm asking you again to marry me, and before you give me one of your standard 'let's think about it,' or 'I've got this or that to do' answers, I want you to know that I talked to Bogie last night and we've both agreed that while you think you're indispensable, your assistant is perfectly capable of taking your place, if necessary, on his next picture."

Despite the frequency of Walter's previous proposals, this one took me by surprise, and events were moving too fast for me. I was numb.

"Take all the time you need to answer," Walter said. "Up to thirty seconds, even. But I won't accept no or maybe."

So this was the surprise, I thought. I also thought about Bogie's praising Walter the night before and his urging me to remember that the surprise was something that he felt I needed. I had been terribly confused those last two or three years; my attraction to Walter was overpowering, but I had been raised, I guess, with the romantic, idealized notion that one can truly love only one person at a time. How the hell could I be in love with *two* men? There just wasn't that much love in anyone. I had tried to convince myself that I really didn't love Walter Thompson—at least not as much as I sometimes felt I did. What a hell of a mess I had created for myself!

I had kept putting off Walter's marriage proposals by stalling, by telling him that I had made a terrible mistake with my first marriage, a mistake that I didn't want to repeat—not just for my sake, but for his, too. I would not marry Walter as a "second choice"; he was too wonderful a man to do that to.

I had first met Walter Thompson in 1950, a year or so after I had divorced my first husband, and a few months after the birth of Bogie's first child. We met at

Prelude

General Services Studio (now Zoetrope Studios) on Las Palmas Avenue, where Walter was producing a film. He asked to take me to dinner, and I accepted. It was the beginning of a five-year friendship and a long-distance, intermittent affair, for although Walter kept an apartment in New York City as his home base, his international movie business enabled him to come home only a few times a year, and then for periods as short as a few days and no longer than a few weeks. And so although Walter proposed to me in 1950—and then again at least once a year for the next five years—his infrequent visits made it easier for me to stall him while I tried to convince myself that although I loved being with him, I wasn't—couldn't—really love him enough to marry him. I convinced myself for a while that one simply can't love two people at once and that if I loved Bogie, which I did, then I couldn't really love Walter. Bogie had seen long before I had that such love was possible, though.

I never told Walter of my relationship with Bogie. Years after we were married I got the impression that he had known—or certainly strongly suspected. But Walter wasn't the kind who gave a damn about the past —his or anyone else's; he was always moving forward, looking forward, and the past didn't matter, except to learn lessons from. As for Bogie, the possibility of our getting married ended with the birth of his children. I knew it then, but wouldn't face it. I knew him well enough to realize that with children in the picture, he would have remained married even to Mayo. That's the kind of man he was. Betty? To be honest, I was jealous of her and looked upon her as a late-blooming interloper in "our" life. Bogie had divorced three times be-

fore Betty came along; a fourth divorce wasn't impossible—in fact, I thought it inevitable until the children
were born.

In the limousine, the engagement ring on my finger,
Bogie's words came back to me. The truth that he had
known all along and that I was too blind to see finally
penetrated my thick skull. I could and did love Walter
Thompson, and he wasn't a second choice. He was another choice, and I loved him dearly.

I began sobbing. Walter put his arms around me and
kissed me. "Hey, come on!" he said. "I realize that I'm
not the world's prize catch, but the prospect of marrying me can't be *that* bad."

I began laughing and sobbing at the same time.
"Bad?" I said. "Walter you're the sweetest, kindest,
most thoughtful, most patient—"

Walter interrupted me, chuckling. "You keep talking
like that and you'll convince me that I'm too good for
you," he said.

"You are," I said, "but you're stuck with me
now. You're lucky to have me for your wife, you
bastard!"

The next couple of minutes were indescribable. I was
suddenly flooded with a happiness that approached a
narcotic state; I was delirious with the joy and the relief
of it. I had been torturing myself for three years and
hadn't realized it until that moment. I remember,
vaguely, Walter laughing and hugging me and talking
a mile a minute. I was so carried away with it all—not
thinking, just feeling—that it seemed forever before
what he was saying to me began registering: ". . . we'll
change at the apartment . . . pick up the Dunbars. . . ."

The Dunbars were mutual friends of ours; Dixie Dunbar was one of my closest friends. "Pick up the Dunbars for what?" I said. I didn't feel like having an engagement party or celebrating with anyone. I just wanted to be alone with Walter.

"To stand up for us," Walter said.

"Walter, we don't even have a marriage license yet. Then there are things like blood tests—are they required in New York?—and—"

"We're not getting married in New York," Walter interrupted. "We're getting married in Richmond, Virginia, where none of that red tape is necessary. I've chartered a plane. The Dunbars are standing by, waiting. I've got a Methodist minister waiting in Virginia—"

"My God, Walter!" I said. "What if I'd said no?"

Walter hugged me and laughed. "I've learned never to take you for granted," he said. "That terrible but distinct possibility is the only reason that the Dunbars are not at this moment sitting in the chartered plane waiting for us at the airport."

Talk about time blurring! We changed, picked up the Dunbars, raced to the airport, flew to Richmond, got married, got back on the plane, flew back to New York, and early that morning, the newlywed Thompsons and the Dunbars, exhilarated but punchy from lack of sleep, were having a champagne breakfast at 21, where we decided to call—and wake—Bogie. He answered, sounding very sleepy.

"Pete?" he said, "Is something wrong?"

"No."

"You crazy broad! Do you know what time it is?"

"I don't even care," I said. "I just got married."

"Good God!" he said. "Walter pulled it off. I never thought you'd do it."

"Well, I did. And now we're celebrating at your favorite spot in the world."

"21?"

"Yup."

"You better put a couple of bottles of their best champagne on my tab there or I'll really be pissed at you two."

"I will," I said.

"Just sign my name, ol' girl," Bogie said. "You always did sign it better than I. Put Walter on the phone, will you?"

"Okay."

"And Pete?"

"Yeah."

"I didn't want you to, and I did—you know?"

"Yes, I know."

"I'm really happy for you."

"Thanks, Bogie. I know you are."

"And don't drink the water. We learned that in Italy, didn't we?"

"What water?"

"Never mind. Put Walter on."

After Walter had talked to Bogie, I asked him about the water. "Oh," Walter said, "that's the surprise."

"I thought *this* was the surprise," I said. "Don't tell me about it; I don't think my nervous system can stand any more surprises. I can't even think."

"Okay," Walter said. He waved for our waiter and said to the Dunbars, "Bogie says for us to have a couple of bottles of Dom Perignon on him. You guys game?"

"Sure," the Dunbars said.

"What surprise?" I said.

"That was nice of Bogie, wasn't it?" Walter said to the Dunbars.

"He's a sweetheart," Dixie said.

"What surprise?" I said.

"I'll bet we woke him," Walter said, looking at his watch.

I grabbed Walter around the neck, pretending to strangle him. "Walter! What surprise?"

Walter and the Dunbars laughed. "What about your delicate nervous system," Walter said. "I don't want my bride suffering cardiac arrest."

"I'm okay now," I said. "I'm a fast recuperater."

Walter took both my hands and held them. "I've cleared my calendar for three months . . ."

He stopped there.

"And? For what?"

"Our honeymoon trip," he said.

"For three months!? Where? Where are we going?"

"Around the world."

It took several seconds for that to sink in. "The world?" I said. "The *entire* world?"

"Well, those explored areas of it."

Walter wasn't exaggerating. He had produced and directed an around-the-world film with Lowell Thomas, and that's when the honeymoon idea struck him. So for the next three months, we traveled to France, Italy, England, Egypt, Thailand, Africa, Lebanon, Arabia, Israel, India, Hong Kong, and Japan. We stopped in Hawaii for a couple of weeks before returning to the United States, and it was there that I received a letter from Bogie, who had been kept abreast of our movements by us and by my assistant.

Bogie's letter was breezy, bringing us up to date on the happenings at the studios. He invited us to sail on the *Santana* with him upon our return and lamented that he hadn't been down to the boat for more than a week. He was scheduled, he said, for some hospital tests. He had had more trouble with his voice and that cough, so the doctors wanted to give him a thorough going-over. "Of course, we know what they're going to tell me," he wrote. "Cut down on the loudmouth and knock off the cigarettes."

He closed by telling Walter to keep his pecker up and by saying that he missed my "smiling, stupid face." And he signed the letter, "Ol' Dad."

We were a bit concerned about Bogie's impending tests but felt sure that his smoking too much was largely the cause of his problems, which seemed slight at the time—just a little cough and occasional minor laryngitis.

But we were very wrong.

15

Sorrow for Ourselves

We returned to California in the spring of 1956 and went straight to my little house in Burbank. Idabell, who had been my housekeeper since my divorce, fixed breakfast for us while Walter made phone calls and I went through the piles of letters and phone messages that had accumulated while I was away. Then I called Bogie. He was in good spirits, and he needled me about what he called my round-the-world hump.

"Next time you guys take a trip," he said, "you ought to get out of the hotels. There's some interesting stuff out there, I'm told."

"You're an incorrigible romantic," I said.

"Yeah, that's what all the women tell me. Listen, how about you and Walter having lunch with me this afternoon? Betty's working, so she can't make it."

"Walter's got a business luncheon," I said, "but I can make it."

"Great. Meet me at Romanoff's at twelve-thirty, and you can bore me with details of your globe-hopping."

Bogie was sitting in his booth when I arrived. He had

just finished a game of chess with Mike Romanoff, and
looked pretty good. He got up and gave me a brotherly
kiss on the cheek; then, as an afterthought, he hugged
me. "You look terrific," he said as we sat down. "I guess
the Old Goat must be taking good care of you."

Mike Romanoff came over and kissed my hand and
congratulated me on my marriage. "The lunch is on me
today," he said.

"Never mind hovering around gloating," Bogie said
to him. "Get us an order of eggs Benedict and a couple
of martinis. That okay with you, Pete?"

"Sounds fine." I looked at Mike. "What did you do,
beat the grouch at chess today?" I said.

"Crushed him," Mike said with a fiendish laugh.

"The bastard cheats," Bogie said.

"One can't cheat at chess," Romanoff said.

"He's lying, Pete. The son of a bitch is playing with
a loaded queen or something."

"A loaded brain," Mike said.

"A full brain, you mean," Bogie said. "And we know
what it's full of. Where the hell are our drinks?"

Mike had our martinis sent over, then went about his
business. Bogie raised his glass in toast. "Here's to your
health and to a happy marriage," he said.

I was touched and said, "Thanks, Bogie."

I guess there must have been a sentimental tone to
my voice, or perhaps it was my expression, but Bogie
gave me a surprised look and said, "Thanks? My God!
The Old Goat is making you civilized. What happened
to my Irish-wetback spitfire? I gotta speak to that husband of yours. You're really boring when you're civil."

I raised my glass and clinked it against his, then
smiled sweetly and said, "Up yours, you ugly bastard."

Bogie laughed. "That's more like it," he said. "For a minute, I thought he'd broken your spirit."

Our food arrived, and we ate and I told Bogie about our honeymoon—too much, probably. I can still talk for hours about that trip. Bogie was attentive and asked questions about certain places, but after a while he seemed distracted, and I thought maybe I was boring him, so I wound down.

"I'm glad you found someone to look after you, Pete," he said. "I worried, you know."

"What for? You know I can take care of myself."

"Yeah, well, I mean about the situation we were in. I'm glad you found someone like Walter, who'll always be there and who'll make you happy. And now that I'm coming unglued, I don't have to worry about you."

"What do you mean, coming unglued?"

"I didn't want to say anything in the letter, but this throat thing—the doctors made a hundred tests, and they found that it's malignant, and . . ."

His words struck me like a blow to the head. I kept thinking, malignant. I don't want to hear it. I don't want to hear any of this. This can't be true.

". . . the doctors think an operation will take care of it," Bogie was saying, "and that I'll be okay."

I kept thinking, no. *No,* this is all a stupid mistake. Bogie couldn't have cancer of the esophagus. The doctors are wrong.

Bogie took a sip of his drink and looked at me. I don't know what my face was registering at the moment, if anything. I couldn't feel for a minute; I was numb.

"Look, kiddo, I really didn't want to tell you this. And we're not going to tell the press or anybody. But the picture will be postponed until I get through with the operation. We can't kid ourselves. We know what this is all about, don't we? If you've got this damn stuff, you've had it. They'll probably cut my throat from ear to ear."

Thank God I finally began thinking again. "There's Oscar," I said, referring to composer Oscar Hammerstein, whom Bogie had visited in the hospital and who had recovered from a bout with cancer. "He made it. Hell, hundreds of people beat it. The medics are doing miraculous stuff now. I know a lot of people who have had cancer and have recovered. They're healthier than ever."

I was praying that he wouldn't ask me to name just two of the "lots of people" who had beaten cancer. There weren't that many in the fifties. Cancer was something that people didn't even discuss in public in those days.

"As for having your throat cut from ear to ear—which, incidentally, I doubt—there are a hell of a lot of people in this town who have been wanting to do that for years. At least you're having it done by *professionals.*"

Bogie chuckled. "Christ!" he said. "I can see that I'll get no sympathy from you! You'll probably volunteer your services to help the doctors do the job."

The subject was changed to a brighter one. Bogie asked me to have Walter call him later that afternoon. "I'd like to talk to him about that production company we've been threatening to form," he said. "Is he still interested, Pete?"

"Are you kidding?" I said. "Who wouldn't be? You know Walter. Of course he's interested."

"When I get through this damn throat thing, I'm

going to be more selective, make better pictures," Bogie said. "And Walter's a doer—not like these god-damned phonies. You know how many genuine people there are in this business? You can count 'em on one hand."

"I'll have him call as soon as he gets home."

"Good. You do that. I'm going to the hospital tomorrow, so I'll be out of commission for a while. Maybe that'll give Walter time to work out some details or something. You guys going to be in town for a while?"

"A few weeks."

"Will you come up and visit me at the hospital?"

"No. I thought we'd take in a movie instead."

"If you get down San Pedro way, check on the *Santana* for me, will you?"

"Sure. But isn't Captain Pete watching her?"

"Yeah. He says she's shipshape, but I'd like a second opinion. She could sink, and he wouldn't tell me—to spare my feelings."

Bogie walked me out to the car. I had found a parking space on Rodeo Drive, near Romanoff's. He leaned through the window and kissed me on the cheek. "I'll see you when they get through carving on me," he said.

"Keep your pecker up," I said cheerfully, though my heart wasn't in it.

Bogie didn't like pity or sympathy. He was the kind who, when he was sick, comforted the well and apologized for the inconvenience his sickness might cause them. Joking with him and holding back my shock at Romanoff's had been hell, and I only made it about three blocks down Wilshire before the tears blurred my vision and I had to pull off the street into a gas station parking lot, where I lost control and wailed.

Cancer was something that happened to strangers, I thought. Not to loved ones. It was a mistake. Bogie wasn't tough enough for cancer. That tough-guy image was a screen invention. Inside, he was soft as a marshmallow. Couldn't people see that? Those goddamned people who criticized him and judged him and didn't even know him? Those poison-pen female columnist bitches who were so stupid that they didn't even know when he was ribbing them and who reported their shit as truth! Dumb broads telling their readers about the "real" Humphrey Bogart and so goddamned stupid that they couldn't find their own asses with both hands.

And Bogie. How could he do this? How could he inflict such pain on *me?* I thought of all the pain-in-the-ass things he had done, all the dumb, childish, juvenile things. All the drink-sodden things. And now cancer?

Was I being punished for loving and marrying Walter?

Crazy thoughts. What the hell was I thinking of? *My* pain? *My* punishment? For a moment, I thought I was going crazy, that they'd have to pack me off to a rubber room. Then all the smart-ass things I had ever said to Bogie came back to me. All the things I had said to him both in anger and in jest suddenly filled me with remorse. How could I have said such things to a man who had cancer? What if he thought I really meant some of them? I thought about the two hours I had just spent with him: Bogie sitting there with cancer inside him, eating away at him, and him sitting there calmly, playing chess with Mike and listening to me chatter away endlessly about India—and with this awful secret inside him.

I was cried out and red-eyed when Walter returned

from his meetings. I told him, and it was a long while before he could get himself to make that phone call to Bogie. But he did.

Bogie had the operation, and after several weeks, he was allowed to go home. He began to get his strength back and was feeling pretty well, although he was undergoing radiation treatments as an outpatient. What he didn't know at the time, because he wasn't told, was that his condition was terminal.

The first time I visited him at home, he was in the upstairs bedroom, in bed. I had a drink with him, and while we were talking, a nurse brought in some food and gave him a little lecture about eating it. When she left, Bogie asked me to flush the food down the toilet. "These damn treatments they're giving me make me nauseated," he said. "I can't eat this damn stuff, and I'm tired of arguing and fighting with these damn nurses."

"How the hell are you going to get your strength back if you flush your vitamins down the toilet?"

"C'mon, Pete! You're sounding just like the nurses. I'll eat this evening, but if I ate everything those crazy broads truck in here every five minutes, I'd look like the Goodyear blimp."

"You promise to eat your dinner?"

"Yes, mama," Bogie mimicked. "Christ! You broads are all *exactly* alike!"

I flushed the food down the toilet, feeling guilty about it, and Bogie said, "I knew I could count on you, ol' girl. Besides, this loudmouth will put lead back in my pencil. Did you bring the shaggy muff?"

"Yes."

"Good. Gotta look pretty for the freeloaders, you know."

"I can cut your hair, and you can use your regular muff," I said.

"Not now. I've had enough people fussing around me and over me in the hospital to last a lifetime. Maybe tomorrow."

Bogie had begun a routine—or, rather, resumed it— that he would continue until his death: his five-thirty cocktail meetings with friends like the Spencer Tracys, John Huston, David Niven, Truman Capote, and other Hollywood regulars. He held the gatherings in the Butternut Room, as usual. At five thirty, he'd be seated, drink in hand, waiting for them to arrive. Later, when he was no longer ambulatory, he had the ceiling removed from the dumbwaiter, which ran between the first and second floors, and used it as an elevator. He'd be taken to it on the second floor by wheelchair and helped onto a stool inside by his nurses; then he'd be lowered to the first floor, where he was helped into another wheelchair and wheeled to the Butternut Room.

Betty and the doctor limited the number of guests and the time they were allowed to stay. But while his strength allowed—which was almost to the day of his death—his freeloader gatherings lasted from five thirty to eight. He always made light of his condition. I never heard him complain. At first, none of his guests knew he was dying; neither did I. But in his last six months or so, most of them, I'm sure, suspected. Still, he'd dress each afternoon in his smoking jacket and sit and talk with them and have a few smashes of loudmouth. And he never showed that he was in pain. His courage and dignity were phenomenal.

Bogie got his strength back after the operation and

was soon strong enough to lounge around the swimming pool. Soon he was going to lunch at Romanoff's again. And eventually he got down to the *Santana,* where he could really relax. When he was on his feet again, Walter and I left for our apartment in New York, where we attended to some business matters. Then about mid-summer 1956, we bought a car and made a leisurely tour of the United States. We called Bogie during our trip, and we were in the Midwest when he told us that he was scheduled for another operation. By the time we returned to Los Angeles, he was home again and recuperating.

We went up to see him and were shocked at his appearance. We both knew then that he was dying. He had lost an awful lot of weight, but he was in good spirits. We told him that we had to leave for Japan, where Walter was producing a picture.

"Listen, you old goat," Bogie said. "You're talking three or four months. How about leaving the kid behind until I get on my feet? She could be a big help, and I could use a few laughs—which looking at her face gives me."

Walter looked at me. "You think you could stand being left behind with the likes of this?" he said.

"Well, provided that he treats me like a lady."

"Damn!" Bogie said. "You're asking an awful lot for a little favor."

"Okay," Walter told Bogie. "But you'd better get on your feet fast. I need her to keep me out of trouble, too, you know."

"I'll be on my feet in no time—maybe a couple of weeks at the most," Bogie said.

Walter went on to Japan, and as we both suspected,

Bogie continuously got worse. He was losing weight so fast that I could hardly believe it. But he kept up his freeloader meetings. I'd put his muff on him and manicure his nails and have smashes of loudmouth with him. It was terrible, though, and I died inside every time I put his toupee on him, he was so skeletal. I know what Betty was going through, for I eventually lost Walter to cancer, too—in 1975.

Bogie never gave up. And he never lost his sense of humor. One evening the doctor came in just as I finished trimming Bogie's hair. Bogie introduced me to him and then talked the doctor into letting me give him a trim, which he badly needed but hadn't had time for. The doctor sat and talked to Bogie as I worked. When I was nearly finished, Bogie began staring at the doctor's hair and shaking his head. We weren't anywhere near a mirror, and the doctor began getting nervous about what I was doing to him. Finally Bogie said, "I don't know, Doc, I guess suggesting that Pete cut your hair wasn't such a hot idea."

"Why?" the doctor said. "What's the matter?"

It had been a long time between ribs, and I was delighted to see Bogie getting into one of them again. I happily went along with him. "Listen, Bogie," I said, "it's not *my* fault! It's been a long time since I've cut someone else's hair. Cutting to fit under a toupee is one thing, but giving a finish cut. . . ." I let the sentence trail off significantly.

"Why the hell didn't you tell us that before you let me talk you into it," Bogie said. "I feel kind of responsible; he hasn't got a muff to cover that mess with, you know. Looks like you put a chamber pot on his head and cut around it. Do you wear a hat, Doc? Forget that. A hat wouldn't help, anyway."

I was trimming around the doctor's ears with the scissors when he jumped to his feet in search of a mirror. I nicked his ear when he jumped, and he was so nervous—and then so relieved when he discovered that I hadn't butchered him—that he didn't even notice.

Bogie laughed like hell when the doctor realized that it had been a joke. The doctor laughed, too, then gave me directions on giving first aid to his ear. "Thanks a lot, Bogie," he said. "If I had jumped half an inch higher, I'd have lost an ear!"

"It couldn't have made you any more ugly," Bogie said.

This happened about a week or so before he died.

There's been a lot of speculation among Bogie's biographers and friends as to whether he knew he was dying. In his autobiography, John Huston describes an uncomfortable moment when Bogie raised the question during one of his cocktail hours in the Butternut Room. Huston was present that evening, as was Bogie's doctor. And Bogie said something like, "Level with me, Doc, am I really going to pull out of this?"

Everyone present held his or her breath until the doctor attributed Bogie's weakness and loss of weight to the treatments he was taking, which was partially true. It seemed to Huston that Bogie accepted the doctor's word. Maybe he did.

Bogie never mentioned death to me. He talked mostly about getting back to work, about getting back to the helm of the *Santana,* and of forming a company with Walter to produce really good films. He seemed to feel that everything would be all right if he could just get his strength back and go to work. But one day, shortly before he died, he said something that made me suspect that he really knew he was dying. We were having a smash in his room, and he suddenly said, "Pete, I'd like you to have the *Santana.*"

It caught me off guard, but I thought fast. "Why, you getting another boat?"

"No. I mean, when I'm done with her."

"Thanks a lot, pal. She'll be worn out and water-logged by the time you're through with her."

"Knock it off, Pete. You know what I mean. I mean if something should happen to me. I'm not gonna live forever, you know. I'd like you to have her."

"You'll outlive us all, you ornery bastard. I appreciate the thought, but you know how my life is with Walter —one day London, the next Timbuktu. Besides, we're living in New York now and thinking of selling the Burbank place—Walter doesn't like it because it's too small."

"You sure you don't want her?"

"I don't need anything, Bogie."

"It was just a thought."

"And an uncharacteristically sweet one, too."

"Well, I *am* a sweet son of a bitch!"

I've often thought of that conversation; it, and the fact that he was down to about ninety pounds, made me sure that he knew. Bogie fought death all the way, but he wasn't stupid. Just brave as hell.

On Saturday evening, January 12, 1957, I told Bogie that I was going out to visit friends on Balboa Island and would be back Monday. Bogie asked me to stop off and check the *Santana,* just to see if Captain Pete needed anything. I told him I would and that I'd call him the next day, which I did.

"Everything's fine," I told him on the phone. "Really."

"What are you doing?"

"Exactly as you suspect. We're down here drinking all your Scotch."

"You bastards," he said, laughing. "I said to check her out, not drink her dry. You tell the captain that there better be a couple of smashes left for me when I get down there. I might pull a surprise inspection."

"I'll tell him," I said. "By the way, the paint job's looking terrific—like new."

Bogie had ordered the *Santana* painted while he recuperated. I didn't think she needed painting, unless she was going to be sold, another thing that made me suspect that he knew.

"I'll bet she looks great," he said. "I can hardly wait to see her. You heading for Balboa now?"

"Just as soon as we run out of Scotch."

"You dirty bastards! You really *are* drinking all my booze! I can put in a call to the harbor cops, you know."

"We'll save you a taste. Captain Pete says he's got the lobster traps out and that he's going to cook a mess of lobster for you like you never saw when you get back down here."

"Put him on the phone," Bogie said.

"I can't. He's on the boat; I'm calling from the clubhouse."

"You tell that bastard to stop threatening me. I've eaten his cooking before."

I laughed.

"She looks really good, though, huh?"

"Terrific. You'll see for yourself soon."

"Yeah. I figure two, maybe three weeks. And tell the captain that I'm gonna count the bottles."

"What bottles? I said we'll save you a *taste.*"

"I believe it."

"I'll see you Monday," I said.

"Monday; right. Keep your pecker up, ol' girl. So long."

Those were Bogie's last words to me. I returned to Burbank early Monday morning, January 14, 1957, and got a call from Natalie Goldberg, Betty's mother. Bogie was dead. He had slipped into a coma Sunday afternoon and had never regained consciousness. He had suffered the night before—the night of the afternoon I had called him from the *Santana*—and had told his doctor that he didn't want to go through another night like that. He didn't. He died peacefully and apparently without pain. That evening I talked to Nat again, and she told me of the funeral arrangements. I cabled Walter, but he couldn't leave Japan.

The memorial service was held at All Saints Episcopal Church on Santa Monica Boulevard in Beverly Hills, Thursday, January 17. The service began at 11:30; everyone was there—except Bogie. In the same hour the memorial service was held, Bogie was being cremated at Forest Lawn a few miles away, in Glendale. The place where Bogie's casket would have been was occupied by the glass case containing his large scale-model of the *Santana*. It was a wonderful touch—Betty's idea, I think. Captain Pete was at the service, too. I sat with Errol Flynn.

The Reverend Kermet Costellano spoke a few words,

then read the Ten Commandments and Tennyson's "Crossing the Bar." Then John Huston read his eulogy, one of the shortest, most touching, and most eloquent I've ever heard. Huston was one of Bogie's few close friends who had known the end was near. He had been told because he was living in Ireland at the time and was very busy, and it was feared that he might not be in the country or able to deliver the eulogy when the dreaded time came. So, I guess, he had been told a few weeks in advance.

Huston must have written and rewritten and honed it to make it the marvelous tribute that it was. Its clean-lined, simple elegance could serve as a model for all eulogies. Among other things, he said of Bogie: "In each of the fountains at Versailles there is a pike which keeps all the carp active, otherwise they would grow over-fat and die. Bogie took rare delight in performing a similar duty in the fountains of Hollywood."

The eulogy was beautifully printed and bound, and each of us at the service was given a copy. I treasure mine.

Bogie had asked to be cremated. He hated the traditional Western funeral, which he considered primitive. Whenever the subject was raised, he would go into a diatribe on what he called the sadistic barbarity with which we in the West merchandize death. "It's hard enough on a guy's loved ones when he kicks off," Bogie used to say. "I mean the shock of it. But then they take the poor son of a bitch away for a couple of days while some half-assed, would-be makeup man plays with his face and makes him look like a clown. Then they stick the poor son of a bitch on public display, like meat in a market, and the loved ones have to go through the shock again, trying also to convince themselves that the clown in the box looks lifelike. This we call civilized!"

It's a sad irony that the "death-merchant lobbyists" got to him in another way. Betty wanted Bogie's ashes taken to sea, where they belonged, but it was against the law in those days. Millions of tons of human waste were dumped into the Pacific daily, but the lobbyists made sure that the pure ash of the cremated was considered unfit for the sea.

Bogie's ashes were placed in a small vault in The Garden of Memory at Forest Lawn. I've visited there occasionally, and I really hate it. I know damn well Bogie would have called it a Disneyland for stiffs. I've often wished that Bogie would be taken to sea now that the law has been changed. It would be far more pleasant to have the whole Pacific as a reminder to those who loved him, rather than that damn walled "garden." The Pacific, midway between the mainland and Catalina Island, is where his heart and spirit was and where he ought to be now.

After the memorial service, Betty held a kind of wake for Bogie back at the house, where Mike Romanoff had set up a buffet and where Bogie's friends could gather for one last freeloaders convention. I helped Nat, Betty's mother, greet people at the door. Betty, in shock, sat out on the lanai amid stacks of cards and cables, numbly poring over them. I could imagine Bogie there, a glass of loudmouth in hand, drifting from one cluster of his friends to another. He would have approved of the "party," but he would have needled everyone for being solemn. "Damn! Let's add a little life to this party. You sons-a-bitches are acting like *you're* the ones who are dead!"

There was some retelling of "Bogie" stories; some self-conscious and restrained laughter about ribs he had pulled. But none of us could quite pull it off, even though we all knew that it was what Bogie would have wanted.

I was doing quite well until Errol Flynn came over and began talking to me. Flynn was really shaken, and his voice trembled. "John's [Houston] eulogy was wonderful, wasn't it, Pete? When he said, 'We have no reason to feel any sorrow for him, only for ourselves for having lost him.' Wonderful. We lost the dearest friend we ever had, Pete."

That got to me, and I made an excuse to visit the kitchen, which was the only place people weren't gathered. It wasn't the smartest move I could have made, though, because May, the cook, was there alone, and crying. She had been with Bogie even during the Mayo days. She had cooked through the Bogart wars. She was nearly incapacitated by Bogie's death. I sought a sanctuary to regain my composure but found a wailing room instead.

As soon as I entered, May threw her arms around me and sobbed, "Oh, Miss Pete, what are we going to do?"

We were hugging and sobbing and trying to console one another when Nat came into the kitchen and discovered us. Natalie Goldberg was a wonderful woman. I had known her and her husband, Lee, for a long time. They'd often had dinner with Walter and me in New York, and they had seen Bogie through to the end, suffering with him and for him. They were gentle and genuine people, and Bogie loved them both.

"Oh, Pete," Nat said, "don't let Betty see you crying.

She'll break down, and she's holding up so well right now."

"Yes. You're right," I said. "I've got to get out of here anyway, Nat. I'll go out the back way."

I kissed May and Nat good-bye. "I'm leaving for Tokyo tomorrow morning," I said. "Say good-bye to Lee and Betty for me."

"I will," Nat said.

I slipped out the back door. In that lovely mansion on Mapleton Drive, time had stopped with death; it had frozen at a dreadful moment that threatened never to pass. Those who have experienced it will know exactly what I was feeling. Leaving that house was something like what I imagine birth trauma to be: like being thrust rudely from the womb into a blinding glare of light and a cacophony of unintelliglble sound—into life. My senses were assaulted by the life beyond Bogie's doorstep. Away from that frozen moment, there was time and the sputtering of a gardener's power mower and barking dogs and traffic on the boulevard and people laughing on the golf links of the Bel Air Country Club nearby. And I was offended. Didn't they know that Humphrey Bogart was dead? What in hell right did they have to be oblivious to that? How insensitive and callous! That absurd thought, too, passed.

People were still arriving to pay their respects as I drove away. I turned east on Sunset Boulevard and drove automatically, as one does on long and hypnotically tedious stretches of highway. My mind was filled with everything and nothing; fragments tumbled in and out of it like colored crystals in a revolving kaleidoscope; meaningless patterns.

I didn't realize that I had crossed the low mountain

range that separates West Los Angeles from the San Fernando Valley to the north. I was suddenly on Barham Boulevard, descending the steep hill and rounding the sweeping curve that opens onto Olive Avenue in Burbank. On my right, separated from the boulevard only by a narrow sidewalk, loomed the huge sound stages of Warner Brothers Studio; they held nothing for me anymore. Across the street sat the Smoke House Restaurant, unchanged in all those fifteen years, and unchanged still.

There was the fleeting, unreasonable notion of going inside the Smoke House to our booth near the bar and ordering us each a smash of loudmouth . . . and waiting. Because none of this had really happened. These past few days were a grotesque rib. Bogie would come in and I'd say to him, "If that drink's too watery, I'll order you another. I just had it set out to keep anyone from joining me before you arrived."

But the Smoke House wasn't where it had all begun. I drove on to my house on Roselli Street; that's where it had really started with us. And I waited there for the frozen moment and the awful night to pass. I sat before the window at which I had first waited for Bogie and watched the light fade. Finally, in the wee hours of the morning—the hours when Bogie used to show up unexpectedly on my doorstep—those flickering mental fragments, which were much like the daily rushes of film, the same out-of-context scenes being played over and over, began taking on a semblance of order. Bogie had always said, "No matter what happens, Pete, they can't say we haven't lived." He had said it so often that I could hear it that night—and even now—as though he had said it only moments ago. I realized what my mind had been groping for, what I knew but couldn't or wouldn't comprehend: that Bogie was gone and that we *had* lived, but now the *we* was gone, too. Now there was just the me of Bogie and me. Now there was only one man in my life. Now there were no doubts or fears about whether I had enough love in me for two. If I had subconsciously held any of my love in reserve from my beloved Walter—and how does one know? How does one measure love?—that, too, passed.

My beloved Walter was waiting for me on the other side of the Pacific; I'd be on my way to him at daybreak. It was with this realization that I finally left the window and went to bed exhausted and was lulled into a peaceful sleep by the secure feeling that Walter was there and that he would take me in his arms and look after me. That was what I wanted. And that was what Bogie had wanted *for* me.

Bogie and I had been so much a part of each other's lives that, in a sense, I feel he took a part of me with him and that a small part of him lives on with me. Let others think what they will; there will always be Bogie and Me.